Country-fied

Life in the Dakotas

by Elaine Babcock

Ellendale, North Dakota

COUNTRY-FIED

Author - Elaine Babcock
Publisher - McCleery & Sons Publishing

Library of Congress Card Number: 00-191663
International Standard Book Number: 0-9700624-2-7
Printed in the United States of America.

Dedicated to my children who encouraged
and supported me always -
Connie Suzanne and Steven Laurance

TABLE OF CONTENTS

Country-fied Experiences

Country-fied Autumn

Country-fied Winter

Country-fied Spring

Country-fied Summer

Country-fied Philosophy

Country-fied isn't like it used to be

Introduction....

The old saying, "You can take the girl out of the country, but you can't take the country out of the girl," is certainly true.

I grew up on the Dakota prairies. I was born in Pierre, South Dakota, lived on a ranch West River until I was 15, then moved with my family to a farm near Monango, North Dakota. Even though I have lived most of my adult life in the small town of Ellendale, North Dakota, my country upbringing continues to influence my thinking, my speaking, and the choices I make.

I was raised in a Christian home so my writing reflects Christian philosophy. Each of my parents had a wonderful sense of humor which when coupled with their faith enabled them to joke even in the face of dire circumstances; for example, when the bank account was down to a couple of dollars, they might say, "We aren't poor. We just don't have any money."

The articles in this book were published in a column called "Country-fied" in the *Dickey County Leader* in Ellendale and in the *Onida Watchman*, Onida, South Dakota.

Many of the articles are about small-town living. The small-town businesses on the Dakota prairies have always depended upon the country people who did their trading on Saturday night. They brought their cream and eggs to town to sell then did their shopping while the children went to a movie. As the rural population decreases and the size of farms increases, small towns are struggling to survive. The old ways are changing and these changes are difficult for rural people to accept.

In my columns I have tried to paint word pictures of the way things used to be and the way I see things now. I have tried to do this with a sense of humor and with empathy and love for the people who, like me, grew up *Country-fied*.

Country-fied Experiences

The Call of Dakota

Every fall the farmers talk.

"The wheat prices aren't too bad this year. Should have planted more."

"If you planted more, the prices would have gone down."

"With a little luck we'll get the sunflowers harvested before a blizzard."

"Too much rain early this spring."

"Not enough later on and then it got hot besides."

"Would have been the best corn crop I ever had. Too bad we got that one streak of hail. Hail the size of baseballs."

The unwritten rule in these conversations is "no optimism allowed and any positive statement must be tempered with a negative."

"Pretty good crops all around this year, but we're in for a tough winter."

"Yah. Don't know why we stay here."

But the farmers know in their hearts why they stay. They love the land. Their roots are tangled with the roots of their ancestors. They are one with the land. They are bound to the land as were their ancestors. Each nationality has its own unique yet universal stories, stories of seeking and yearning for a better life on the land.

Next spring we will hear the farmers say, "It's got to be better this year," as they begin to repair their machinery and start planning which crops to plant. That's the way it is. That's the way it has always been. They know, even as they complain about the hardships and the struggles that there is no life they would rather have.

Dakota women are historically strong. They work beside their husbands in farming the land and earning a living. In addition to their strength and determination, they add touches of gentleness and beauty in times of bleakness and adversity. Some display a quiet acceptance of life's circumstances. Others fight with a toughness that refuses to accept defeat. Their love of the land is as deep as that of their husbands.

Next spring as the farmers till the soil, their children will peel off shoes and socks. They will feel the warmed earth against the soles of their bare feet as they run. They will reach down to scoop up mounds of dirt and let it slip through their fingers.

They, too, feel the promise of life that the soil holds. Even the children sense God's spirit in the pulse and rhythm of the land.

As they grow older the children toil and sweat beside their parents and so another generation learns to appreciate and respect the land and the spirit of Dakota.

Quilting

My great-grandmother quilted. I still have one of her red, white and blue quilts, every tiny stitch done by hand. I think she would be pleased to know that her great-great-grandson pulls that one off the shelf whenever I'm not paying attention, and curls up under it. She has left a priceless piece of her history in that quilt.

My grandmother made a hand-appliqued Orange Blossom quilt. It was stored in the old black trunk on the porch. It was never used because it was "too good to use." Another chapter of history is related in that quilt.

The quilts my mother made were practical, thick, and warm. She quilted more from a sense of necessity than she did for pleasure and beauty. I snuggled under the dark wool patchwork with the plaid flannel back and felt cozy and secure in the cold Dakota night. Her story of living through the Depression was told in the making of something from whatever she had at hand.

I quilt for a combination of reasons. I can't bear to throw anything away if there is some part of it still usable, so I make quilts out of the good parts of denim jeans. Remnants of clothes I've sewed for my children make memory quilts for them. T-shirt logos get fused, serged, and appliqued onto sheets. I quilt for missions, and I quilt to make something beautiful for myself.

Until a few years ago, I made practical, somewhat symmetrically balanced quilts with half-inch seams that would stand up under dozens of washings.

Then I went to some quilting classes where I learned the "right" way to do them with one-fourth inch seams pressed in the same direction instead of open. I started thinking about color, design, geometric shapes, and fancy borders. For the first time in my life, I bought fabric for the express purpose of making a quilt instead of using remnants or recycled fabrics. I started to look at quilting as an art form.

I went to quilt shows where every quilt was more spectacular than the one before it. It was better than a Fourth of July fireworks display. I went into a two-month depression because my quilts were not works of art like those I had seen. They just didn't measure up.

Then I chastised myself and thought, "It doesn't really matter. You love quilting, and who says your quilt has to be a Monet? Who says the corners all have to meet perfectly? If the back has bulges and tucks in it, who cares? It's MY quilt and I can make it however I want to make it."

I started quilting again.

My daughter has made quilts for her Grandpa, her parents, her brother, her cousins and for her special friends. When she started quilting, her quilts had half-inch seams and the corners didn't match perfectly. But they were beautiful and we all loved our quilts because she made them. The more she quilted, the more intricate her quilts became with their quarter-inch seams, hundreds of tiny triangular pieces and dazzling, vivid colors that reflect her personality. We love those quilts also.

They are a continuation unto the fifth generation of an art form that will never die.

May I Have Your Recipe, Please?

On a scale of 1 to 10, my cooking talents probably rank a negative 10. It isn't that I haven't tried.

When my two sisters and I were kids, we were always stirring up something and proudly presenting it to Dad for compliments at suppertime. He graciously ate our experiments and was good at praising our efforts. But he really had to struggle to find something positive to say about the chocolate cake I baked. He said, "This is very good. The next time you bake one, beat it a little longer, and the white streaks will disappear."

He ate another piece, just to prove it tasted good.

Then there was the horrible chicken casserole I concocted with cut-up chicken, bread crumbs, and other ingredients, which fortunately I can't remember. Dad took a hefty portion and valiantly ate it as I watched him and waited for his compliment. Finally he said, "You worked hard on this casserole, didn't you, honey?"

I beamed and said, "Yes, I did, Daddy."

When I grew up and had my own family, I wanted them to enjoy pancakes like my mother made. They were wonderful, fluffy, golden brown, done-in-the middle pancakes. I asked her for her recipe. She said, "Start with flour."

"How much flour?" I asked.

"It depends on how many people want pancakes."

"What next?"

"Some baking powder."

"How much?"

"It depends on how much flour you used."

"Of course. What else?"

"Beat in a couple of eggs, three if they're pullet eggs. And buttermilk if you've just churned."

"Sure, Mom. I churn at least once a week."

"Regular milk will do. But if you use buttermilk, put in a little soda."

"How much milk do you use?"

"Enough to make it look right."

"Thanks, Mom. I'll try making pancakes sometime."

And I did. With a little help from Aunt Jemima.

I asked Grandma for her recipe for Thanksgiving cookies. Hers were so tasty - soft and spicy. I made them, following her recipe exactly as she wrote it. My cookies hit the cooling rack like North Dakota rocks hitting a flat-bed trailer. My kids were thankful when I quit trying to make Thanksgiving cookies. I swear Grandma gave me the wrong instructions just so everyone could say, "Nobody makes cookies like Grandma."

My dear friend used five recipe cards to detail the exact measurements for the ingredients and step-by-step-you-can't-get-it-wrong directions for baking bread. Bless her heart, she really had faith in me. I had a day off so I thought, "Why not?"

I got out the five recipe cards. I sifted, measured, melted, dissolved in lukewarm water, let set, beat till fluffy, kneaded, let rise, punched down, kneaded, let rise, punched down, shaped, greased, let rise, baked, brushed with melted butter. My friend forgot to tell me to chisel the sunken loaves out of the pan and sharpen the saber saw for slicing. Maybe someone will give me an electric bread maker for my birthday.

I thought, "Surely I can make something out of the children's cookbook. Ah, yes. Easy as 1-2-3 Peanut Butter Rice Krispy Bars."

I pulled a sample of the sticky, gooey mess out of the pan. It didn't look promising. I said, "Here, Woofer, have a treat."

She wagged her tail in anticipation as I put a chunk of it in her dish. She took a big bite and her little jaws clamped tightly together. She whimpered and ran behind the couch. From that day on she eats nothing in her dish except her out-of-the-bag Woofie Biscuits.

I have learned not to trust a recipe that has "Never-fail" as part of the title. I made the Never-fail Pecan Log at Christmas time. It sounded so easy. I mixed the easy-to-assemble ingredients, shaped them into beautiful little "logs," and rolled them in chopped pecans. When I checked them a half-hour later, they were flat little pools in the bottom of the pan. I reshaped them, put them in the freezer, and quickly cut them in slices when I took them out. But, alas, once again when they hit room temperature the slices liquified. I gave my family bowls of ice-cream, stuck a spoon in the "Never-fail Pecan Log" and told them I had tried a new recipe for butterscotch topping.

Actually, not being a good cook has its benefits. When we are planning a family picnic and I say, "What shall I bring?" I secretly hope someone will suggest that I might furnish a watermelon or hot dogs and paper plates. They usually do.

I don't have to waste a lot of time writing my recipes on cards and trying to tell people how I make something, because nobody ever asks me. If anyone is so foolish as to ask me for a recipe, I just say, "You can never trust a skinny cook."

That they believe!

The Joys of Being Directionally Challenged

Traveling is not something I do well and it isn't on my list of priorities for my retirement years. I often opt for staying home rather than going places for two major reasons. I have suffered from motion sickness all my life and I am usually lost.

When I have to drive into a large city, I write to the Chamber of Commerce and order a map at least three weeks before I'm scheduled to go. I find the location of my destination and spend several hours figuring out exactly which route to take. I write down the highway numbers and the street names. Since I suffer from lefturnaphobia, I carefully figure out how I can avoid all left turns which means that sometimes I have to make three rights to make a left. Sometimes I have to take an alternative route even though it means traveling 25 miles out of my way.

When I'm fortunate enough to have a map reader in the seat beside me, I say such intelligent things as, "Point me in the right direction. I'll find it eventually. How can you tell me which direction to go? You're facing south and the top of the map is north. Doesn't that confuse you? Does the map show whether I go over or under to get onto interstate? I'm not lost, I'm just not quite sure where I am."

Sometimes my map reader gets impatient and says, "You should remember how to get there, you've been there before," to which I respond, "Sure, I've been there before. But I didn't know where I was when I was there before."

I don't understand people who always know which direction is east and which is south no matter where they are. My "west" can become "north" while I'm going the same direction. I'm fortunate if it's high noon and the sun is shining. At least I know for sure which direction is south. And if I'm driving in Colorado, I know that the Rockies are to the west, unless, of course, I'm *in* the Rockies. Then how do I know?

My daughter has inherited my talent for directions. If someone tells her to turn left, she looks at her hands, notes the large gold ring on the index finger, and points the car in that direction. I don't wear rings, so it's anybody's guess as to which way I'll turn.

I never admit to anyone that I was lost, but my family members all know that if I say, "I took the scenic route," I didn't have a clue as to my whereabouts. But I've met such interesting people and I've seen such interesting things by being lost. When I was lost in the Black Hills, I stopped three times to ask directions. I met loggers, hunters, and other tourists. All three groups tried to give me complete and accurate directions, but none of them made any sense.

After several tries, I arrived where I had intended to arrive, but if I had found my way on the first attempt, I'd have missed seeing that gorgeous waterfall and would never have taken my best- ever black-and-white photo of the walking bridge.

Actually I don't mind being lost if I'm not alone, don't have a deadline to meet, and if I can maintain my sense of humor. Some of my most memorable "quality times" with my son have been the times when we've been lost together.

When Steve was ten years old we drove to Fargo to stay with friends for the week-end. As usual, there was road construction in Fargo and I had to take a detour. Now that was really confusing when I didn't know where I was before I took a detour. After I had driven for quite awhile Steve said, "Well, Mom, if you ever wanted to see rural Minnesota, we've arrived."

At least I didn't damage the car when I was driving in Fargo like I did when I went to a play at the LaMoure Summer Theater. I missed the road construction detour sign entirely and drove in the dark for two miles on piles of loose gravel and large rocks. My car was not happy with me and my mechanic asked me why I was averse to driving on smooth pavement.

Even in places where I know where I am because I've been there a hundred times, I can miss a turn because I'm simply not paying attention. I have been known to drive past my own driveway and end up cruising along on Cemetery Road. That's really embarrassing if I have a friend in the car with me. If I have one of my relatives in the passenger seat, they just laugh and add another chapter to their family joke books.

Driving is boring and my mind gets restless, so sometimes I'm creating a story while I drive. Some of my best stories are born that way and if I don't write them down right away, I might forget, so I find a scrap of paper or a checking account deposit ticket in my purse and scribble the idea down. This writing with one hand and driving with the other can be a dangerous business.

For someone as confused as I am just getting into a vehicle is a dangerous business. God must be shaking His head and saying, "There she goes again! Come on, Angels. A little more overtime today."

I Always Cry in Airports

While people-watching in airports, I can only guess at their stories. As passengers arrive and depart there are tears of joy and tears of sorrow and I usually cry in sympathy as I pretend not to be watching.

I watch the young marine hugging his mother and giving his father a manly farewell handshake. Mother's tears are visible but the men are smiling bravely, as men are supposed to do. The marine has to be at least 18 years old, but he looks like a child. I wonder where he is going and think, "What if this is the last time his parents see him?"

I see tiny tots running and screaming, "Grandma! Grandma! What did you bring us?" She swoops them up, kisses them soundly, and digs in her pockets for peppermints.

The well-dressed man paces the floor till the plane lands and he sees the light of his life floating down the ramp to meet him. He hands her the red rose he was hiding behind his back and her eyes dance.

Then I hear the announcement for an unattended minor to board. Sobbing, she clings to her mother. The mother's tears are running in rivulets as she gives her daughter one more hug and sends her with an attendant to board the plane. I can only guess at the reasons for the separation.

I think my daughter almost hates to come home. Every time I meet her at the airport I cry, tears of joy. Every time I take her to the airport to leave I cry again, tears of sadness. That's just how it is and I sometimes embarrass my family by being so emotional.

On my first flight, I flew alone with my baby girl to Denver. I was afraid of being motion sick, afraid of taking off, afraid of changing planes and afraid of landing. I was on a champagne flight and I couldn't even have champagne because I was a minor! When I got into the Denver airport I walked briskly and pretended to know where I was going. It's not easy to look worldly-wise and sophisticated while carrying a baby, a diaper bag, a huge purse, a garment bag, and a piece of luggage.

Airport waits can also cause tears of frustration. I once had a five hour wait in an airport with my young, hyperactive boy. For him, all new situations and surroundings required immediate and intense investigation. He checked out the bathroom, the cigarette butts in the large metal sand-filled ashtrays, put money in the peanut machine, helped an old man carry his luggage, asked me to read him the funnies, put money in the gum machine, climbed on my lap for a hug, checked out the doors that open without being touched, offered two teenagers pieces of gum, got a drink from the fountain after seeing how high the water would go, talked to the baggage checkers, put more money in the peanut machine, played peek-a-boo with a fussy baby to make her laugh, tried to pet a yipping puppy in a carry-on. And all of this was accomplished in the first hour. I (and everyone else in the airport) started praying that he would have a long nap.

Although I still don't qualify for frequent flyer discounts, air travel has become easier with experience and I'm no longer afraid of flying. But there is still an excitement and a mystery as I near an airport and begin to think of all the stories being lived by people who cross my path just once in my lifetime.

If I Had a Hammer

I just finished hanging a picture. I pounded the nail into the wall with the handle of a butcher knife.

Once upon a time I had a hammer. In fact I had three hammers, a hammer with a wooden handle, a hammer with a metal handle, and a tack hammer. And they were all in my beautiful little red tool box along with a set of six screw-drivers, a 50-foot steel tape, three pairs of pliers, four C-clamps, a monkey wrench, a square, a box of assorted nails, a container of screws, and a pair of tin snips.

Then I was blessed with a son, a curious son who was born with his motor running. Before he could walk, he was checking things out. Electrical outlets had to have covers, and anything smaller than a bread box had to be put on top of cupboards. At age three he was walking around with a screwdriver in his hand saying, "Mom, give me something to take apart and put back together. Let me take your radio apart and put it back together."

One day I found my box of sewing machine attachments, or rather, what used to be sewing machine attachments. Each and every attachment had been completely dismantled down to unrecognizable pieces. How had he managed to do that much damage without being caught in the act? He knew he would be punished if I caught him "fixing" my possessions, but any possible punishment was apparently worth the risk.

Once in awhile I take my little red tool box out of the closet and look at it with fondness. There's no need to open it. There hasn't been a tool in it for twelve years.

The wrenches are somebody's lawn ornaments. The pliers are probably in the basement where they were used to repair a fishing rod. The hammer might be in my son's room where he used it when he was hanging a shelf for his tapes. My pair of knife-edged dressmaking scissors is a permanent passenger in a friend's vehicle in which he helped to wire a stereo. Why would he use my good scissors? He couldn't find the wire cutters, of course!

Last month I almost got even. I was repairing my lawn mower with a kitchen mallet, a nail file, and a bottle opener. But I could find nothing that even closely resembled a pair of pliers. I thought, "Ah, Steve's tackle box. I know he has a pair of slim-nosed pliers in there!"

I opened his gorgeous tackle box in which every lure, lead, bobber, and scaler were lined up in absolute order and there they were! A beautiful, shiny pair of red slim-nosed pliers.

With a gleam in my eye and malice in my heart, I used those beautiful red slim-nosed pliers to pull the tangled cord out of my lawn mower. When I finished using them, I threw them under the back porch to rust and ruin in the rain.

And I didn't feel one twinge of guilt.

Driving Lessons

Dan was excited. Finally he was old enough. He said, "Dad, will you write me a check for driver's education at the high school?"

"Now wait a minute, Son. There's no reason why I can't teach you to drive. I know everything there is to know about driving and just think of the money we will save."

Dan didn't care who rode with him as long as he had wheels. After all, it was a piece of cake. He already knew almost everything there was to know about driving.

Saturday came. Dad had barely closed his door when Dan slammed the car into reverse, lurched out of the garage, spun around the yard, pushed the accelerator to the floor board as he left the driveway, and didn't signal when he turned onto the gravel road.

As they were cruising on the township road, dust flying, gravel stones pounding the car, Dad said, "Slow down, Son, you're going to rear-end somebody."

Suddenly Dad yelled, "DEER!"

Dan whipped the car into the left ditch, avoiding the deer. He flew over an approach, narrowly missing a culvert and a telephone pole, and swerved quickly back onto the right side of the road. He did all of this while he was fine-tuning the stereo and adjusting the rear-view mirror. He grinned and said, "Wow! I really handled that well, didn't I?"

Dad could only grunt as he pushed his glasses back onto the bridge of his nose and reached over the seat to retrieve his cap.

When they screeched to a halt in front of the house, Dad got out of the car, shook out his right knee which was stiff from helping Dan brake, went into the kitchen and said, "Mama, get the checkbook. This boy needs driving lessons."

Two years later, Cora was ready for driving lessons. Dad was certain that he could handle giving shy, cautious Cora instructions.

On the appointed Saturday, Cora got ready. Dad sat in the car and waited, waited while she adjusted the mirrors, the seat position, the seat belts, then adjusted them again, just to be sure they were right. He waited while she took a full 30 seconds to find drive. Then as Cora crawled along, hugging the edge of the road to be safe, Dad said, "Step on it, Cora, we're going to be rear-ended!"

Cora crept along at seventeen miles-per-hour with her left foot riding the brake. Then she stopped the car entirely to let a turtle cross the road.

After the turtle was safe in the tall grass on the edge of the road, Cora grinned and said, "Aren't you glad I saved the turtle's life, Dad?"

Dad said, "Step on it, Cora. We've backed up traffic clear back to the old Johnson place. Doesn't all that honking bother you?"

When they finally rolled to a stop in front of the house, Dad got out of the car, shook out his right knee which was stiff from helping Cora step on the gas, went into the kitchen and said, "Mama, get the checkbook. This girl needs driving lessons."

Two years later the twins, Hayley and Clem approached Dad about driving lessons. Dad leaned back in his recliner, put his feet up, snapped his fingers and said, "Mama, get the checkbook. These kids need driving lessons."

No Dogs Allowed

The little plastic dishes were lined up on the sidewalk. They contained water, leftover chunks of roast beef, mashed potatoes, and sandwich meat.

"What's going on here?" I asked my young son when I came home from work.

He said, "This little dog likes me. I'm going to keep her. She needs a good home."

"Steve, you know we can't have a dog. I've never liked to have animals in the house. There would be dog hair all over everything, she'd wake us up in the night with her barking. It costs a lot to feed and care for a dog. You're in school all day and I'm at work. Who would take care of her?"

"I'll let her out when I come home for lunch. I'll feed her and give her water."

"That's not the half of it. Dogs get sick. It costs money to take them to the vet. They have to have their rabies shots and a dog license. Who will pay those expenses?"

"I'll pay for her shots out of my own money. Please, Mom, let me keep her. The neighbor doesn't want her and she needs a home. Please, Mom, please," Steve pleaded.

"No, Steve. You can't keep her and that's final. I don't want to hear another word about this dog."

The first night of Bozo's stay with us, she curled up to sleep at the foot of Steve's bed. When I went to the kitchen to fix breakfast the next morning, I discovered a mountain of paper in the middle of the living room, and Bozo slunk behind the couch. She knew she had done a bad thing by chewing up every newspaper in the magazine rack.

"Steve, look what your dog has done," I said. "You will have to clean up the mess, then take the dog back. We can't keep her if she's going to be this destructive."

"I'll clean it up. She won't do it again, I promise."

Steve cleaned it up, and somehow she must have understood my threat. She never chewed paper again.

Bozo was a cute little dog, a fox terrier cross. Every afternoon when it was nearing the time for Steve to come home from school, she would put her nose under the curtain and her paws on the window sill, and watch for him to come bounding up the sidewalk. As soon as she saw him, she wagged her tail, she danced, she leaped, she yipped for joy. She scratched at the door until he put her leash on her to take her outside. He hopped on his bike and the dog ran like the wind behind him.

No matter how quietly I sneaked into the kitchen and opened the refrigerator, she was there before I closed the door, begging for her share of the snack. If I sat in the rocking chair, before I could pick up my book or my knitting, she was on my lap hoping I would give her a few crumbs of affection and a little scratching behind her ears.

Eventually I got used to vacuuming up dog hair and cleaning food dishes on a daily basis. Even though she was purely annoying, I realized that she was good for Steve. He didn't have to come home to an empty house and if no one else listened to him or cared about him, she was there with her undivided attention.

One day I was sick and made my bed for the day on the couch. She leaped up on me, licked my face, and whimpered as if in sympathy.

When Steve came home and saw her curled up on my cold feet, he said, "Now aren't you glad we have a dog?"

I said, "Yes, I have to admit, I'm glad we have her. I must be really sick!"

Painting

I would never be able to earn a living cooking, singing, fitness training, or truck driving. Add to that list painting as in painting a room, a piece of furniture or the exterior of a house.

I have also been asked not to volunteer my painting skills at church or for any charity work. I volunteered once and someone came behind me and repainted the wall I had done.

Last year my daughter, bless her kind, loving heart, painted my kitchen, living room and hallway. She's tall enough to reach the ceiling with a roller while she's standing on the floor. She saved me hours of agony which I'd have endured climbing up and down a ladder while balancing paint buckets, brushes, or rollers.

When I was married, my husband watched me paint until he could stand it no longer. Then he said, "You're painting like a woman. You're scrubbing with the paint brush. Here, let me show you how."

He took the brush and I disappeared into my sewing room.

One week-end recently I decided to tackle the kitchen cupboards. They were in sad need of a varnish job.

Of course, I couldn't just varnish the cupboards. They needed to have all of the contents removed, shelves scrubbed, and the accumulated grease and grime removed from the doors. I tried three products guaranteed to remove grease and discovered that the only thing that really worked was elbow grease. I emptied all of the drawers sorting the contents into baskets to save and piles to throw. The stove and refrigerator had to be pulled out so I could clean behind them. This is not a job for the faint-hearted.

Through this entire chore, I walked on crunchy remnants of cereal flakes, stray grains of rice, and chunks of pretzels and rotelle. How could I sweep with all the stuff piled in the middle of the kitchen?

I bravely tackled the challenge of the varnish. After a half-hour, I had varnish on my hands even though I wore thin rubber gloves, varnish on the soles of my feet even though I was wearing sandals, varnish in my hair even though I was wearing a scarf. I used a drop cloth, but I still had varnish on the floor, on the countertop, on the wall, and on the toaster and kettles.

My son walked in, surveyed my mess, and said, "Mother, you're painting like a woman. You're scrubbing with the paint brush. Here, let me show you how."

"Aha! It's in the genes!"

I handed him the brush and disappeared into my sewing room.

Rummage Sale Addictions

I hate auction sales.

I've never quite figured out when I'm supposed to nod my head or raise my hand and have been known to raise my own bid on an item I didn't know I had put a bid on. Any piece of furniture that I want goes way over my budget and I don't like antiques, a fancy word for over-priced stuff I grew up with which I didn't like when I was growing up with it.

Rummage sales are worse.

One of my friends was wearing a stunning dress. When I complimented her on it, she said she bought it at Sally's. I said, "I'm not familiar with that store."

She laughed and said, "Salvation Army."

I never seem to find the kind of wonderful bargains that my friends and relatives find. I'm the one who will buy the pair of pants which appears to be in perfect condition, then when I get them home discover that the price tag has been taped over a gaping hole in the knee.

The shiny toaster that looks brand new and is in the original box hisses, sizzles, and shoots sparks when I plug it in.

I once bought a size 12 blouse in its plastic wrapper and when I tried to put it on, realized it was a girl's size 12.

A friend of a friend takes her cellular phone with her when she goes to rummage sales so she can call other family members to alert them to good deals on items they may need. Talk about a networking concept!

Be careful when riding in a car driven by a rummage sale addict. That car will automatically brake and make a left turn whenever it sees a rummage-sale sign.

I'm amazed when I see people scour every rummage sale in town, then four months later have their own rummage sale. When I think about having a rummage sale myself, I find nothing that I consider good enough to put on public display.

One Saturday, years ago, I cleaned my entire house and got real serious about simplifying my lifestyle. I intended to put all of the "good stuff" that someone might want into boxes and have a big rummage sale.

At the end of the week, I had one grocery bag full of stuff. The stuff I had was stuff I could still use, or stuff my children might want someday. I realized that I use my stuff until it's worn out and the only fitting place for it is garbage can heaven.

The only time I had a rummage sale, it was advertised to open at 8:30 a.m. At 7:00 a.m. I had the wits scared out of me when I looked up and saw two women, noses to the glass, peering through the picture window to see what I was putting price tags on.

That cured me for life.

Time for Tea

I wonder how many cups of tea my teatime friends and I have had together. We drink tea in the shade on the deck when the temperature is 100 degrees. We drink tea from insulated mugs while sitting in a cozy kitchen when it's 20 below. If the sink is full of dirty dishes, we drink tea from paper cups.

Good news is enhanced with a tangy spice and bad news is softened with a cup of sweet soothing lemon.

When we have financial blessings we share extravagant gourmet blends and savor every drop. When money is scarce we have generic and can scarcely tell the difference.

Coffee was the main beverage in our home when I was growing up, but if I was sick or had a bad cold, Mother brewed green tea in a black teapot etched with gold. I felt better immediately as I sipped the healing tea from a plain white coffee mug.

Perhaps I felt better simply because she gave me that extra attention as she felt my forehead to see if I had a fever, but maybe the tea had healing properties which at that time had not been researched or identified. Mother just knew that it made me feel better.

Centuries ago the Chinese discovered that people who drank tea were healthier than those who did not. Perhaps it was simply because they boiled their water to make the tea, but perhaps they were on to something about the beneficial effects of tea even though they didn't understand why or how it worked.

Recent studies reported in *Prevention Magazine* and *Reader's Digest* claim that tea contains biochemical compounds called polyphenols which include flavonoids. The flavonoids are antioxidants which may aid in preventing cell damage contributing to a number of diseases including strokes, heart attacks, and some types of cancer.

The three major types of tea are black, oolong, and green. The difference in them is in the processing with green tea having the shortest time of processing, black the longest, and oolong somewhere in between. All three types are said to be beneficial.

Imagine that! Something I really like is actually good for me.

Several natural product companies now manufacture a green tea supplement in capsule form so that those who don't have enough time to sit down to drink several cups of tea per day can still receive the benefits of it. Somehow, that just wouldn't be quite the same as sitting down in my favorite chair with a cup of steaming tea beside me as I read the morning paper or a chapter of a good book. A capsule certainly couldn't replace the flavor of a carefully brewed cup of tea sipped in the company of a special friend.

Worthy Work

There are many references to work and good works in the scriptures.

Colossians 3:23 says, "Whatever your task, work heartily, as serving the Lord and not men."

In Acts 9, Tabitha was raised from the dead so she could continue her good works and acts of charity in serving others.

Ecclesiastes 5:18 says, "Behold, what I have seen to be good and to be fitting is to eat and drink and find enjoyment in all the toil with which one toils under the sun the few days of his life which God has given him, for this is his lot."

We were created to do good works, born to use the unique talents and abilities which God chose to give each of us. Perhaps that is why we feel a restlessness in our spirits when we are not doing what we were called to do.

How do we know what our vocational calling is? Wouldn't it be easy if God just wrote it in the sky or appeared to us in a dream? He doesn't do that often, of course. God expects us to figure it out with the intelligence and discernment we have.

Our society places more value on persons in certain kinds of work than others. Are we proud of a son or daughter who is a doctor? Are we equally proud of a son or daughter who is a sanitation worker? Both are functioning in serving positions. Both are doing necessary and important work. We would quickly value the sanitation workers if they went on strike and the garbage piled up on our boulevards for a couple of months.

A family might rather have mother dress up and look pretty when she sits behind a desk in an office than to have her dress in work denims, heavy socks and work shoes to weld and solder in a factory. Perhaps she hates answering the phone, keeping schedules and filling out forms, and loves the sense of accomplishment she gets from creating things and running machinery. She might be valued more for a pretty job even though the non-glamorous job earns her an extra $4 an hour.

Why is our society willing to pay football players and actresses who play trashy parts in movies millions of dollars while elementary school teachers barely make enough to support a family? Which job is more important and what does that tell us about our values?

The work ethic in America is changing rapidly. Years ago, people were considered successful if they remained in the same job or business for thirty or forty years. Now people can expect to change jobs or careers an average of seven times in their working years. Change is stressful. Change is difficult. We have to be adaptable and flexible. We can look forward to downsizing and restructuring and perhaps periods of unemployment. Those time are difficult, indeed, and unemployed people are not always treated kindly.

If someone is sick or there is a death in the family, the church and community come forward with their help and their support. If someone loses a job, that person is often criticized or condemned and left alone to work out his own problems. The unemployed person may be in a state of great anguish and dealing with intense feelings of worthlessness and despair.

He is not happy because he knows he was created for good works. He is probably in desperate need of some understanding friendship and the assurance that God values him whatever his circumstances.

Wouldn't it be wonderful if all people could be in jobs they love, in jobs for which they have God-given talents? Wouldn't it be wonderful if employers and employees could respect and value one another and work together toward a common goal?

If we can't find a job that suits us exactly or maybe we are in a job we hate, we can still be thankful for God's provision in the job we have.

Perhaps we can learn to like the job we have while we work on some honest self-evaluation which helps us find our niche.

Third Shift Soliloquy

Third shift workers are those people who you know exist but you never see them. They are the hotel desk clerks, nurses, medical transcriptionists, convenience store clerks, factory workers, disc jockeys, etc. etc.

When you are sleeping, they are working. When you are working, they are trying to sleep. They turn the ringers off on their telephones and you can talk to them only on their answering machines and if you are lucky, they will return the call and leave a message on *your* answering machine. You might meet them when you are going and they are coming, or perhaps when you are coming and they are going.

They have no life. At least no life that you can see because nothing they do meshes with what you do.

It's a lifestyle that cannot be understood unless it has been experienced.

Strange things happen to their sense of time and place. It's not at all unusual for one of them to say, "What day is this? Is this Tuesday or Wednesday, and if it's Wednesday is it *our* Wednesday or is it really Tuesday?"

They start work on Sunday night but it's actually counted as Monday, so they have their Monday over with before most of the world wakes up and says, "Oh, no! It's Monday already."

People say, "Good morning," to their co-workers when they go in at

10 p.m. which makes sense to them because their co-workers are disoriented as well.

Their main topic of conversation in the break room is the amount of sleep they got or didn't get the day before, the various circumstances which prevented them from getting enough sleep, and how many days their kids are grounded for waking them up too soon, or in some cases, not waking them up soon enough and they were late for work.

If they start babbling or saying things that don't make any sense at about 4 a.m. everyone knows they are just trying to keep themselves awake. They joke and say, "You don't have to make sense. We understand it anyway. We work third shift."

Time disoriented third shift workers often wake up at six o'clock and don't know if it's six a.m. or six p.m.

They come home from work at 7 a.m. which seems like the end of the day instead of the beginning of the day, so they have hotdish and salad for breakfast. They wonder why the garbage hasn't been picked up yet, then they remember that the garbage collector comes at noon but their body clocks say, "It's suppertime."

If this article doesn't make any sense to you, it's probably because you have never been a third shift worker. Maybe you can find a third shift friend or relative who can help you understand this strange phenomenon.

I'll bet you will have to leave a message on their answering machine.

What's Wrong with Ordinary?

I play the piano.

I don't play the piano well. In fact, I play so badly that my son laughs at me and the dog runs under the bed. My rocking tenths are too slow and I forget to lower the third in a minor chord. If I practiced the simplified version of "Rhapsody in Blue" for three hours a day for a month, I still wouldn't be able to play it the way George wrote it. I play the piano anyway. Sometimes I'm even so bold as to sing. I'm even less talented at singing than I am at playing the piano. In fact, my singing is so bad that the dog howls and my son leaves home. I sing anyway. If I'm depressed the music chases my blues away. If I'm tired, it energizes me. It washes away my anger if I'm upset. It's therapy-free of charge-and the quality of the performance is immaterial.

When I was in high school, I avoided taking chemistry because I was afraid that I wouldn't be able to understand it. Maybe I wouldn't have understood it, but maybe I would have enjoyed the subject. Maybe I could have been so good at it that I'd have chosen a career that would have changed my whole life. I'll never know. Out of fear of being ordinary, I missed the opportunity of finding out.

I have a sister who *cooks*. She doesn't just cook, she *cooks*. Her meals look like pictures in a magazine. Her table is gorgeous, beautifully decorated with foods prepared in new and unusual ways. Eating in her home is not just eating, it's an experience. I was once lamenting to my dad as we were eating plain scalloped potatoes and pork chops in my kitchen that by comparison with my sister, I was a failure at cooking. He said, "Your sister is a good fancy cook. You are a good plain cook and that's important, too."

Thanks, Dad. I needed that. Thanks for reminding me that it's okay to be ordinary!

I become extremely frustrated in doing anything in the line of household repairs or upkeep. Put a screwdriver or a hammer in my hand and I'm on my way to creating a disaster, or hurting someone severely. But I unplugged my daughter's bathroom sink and painted my house. I hated every minute of scraping and sweating in the sun but I did it!

God gave me many ordinary talents. I'm not exceptional at ice-skating, interior decorating, housecleaning, telling jokes, dancing, math, public speaking, balancing a budget, saving money, or entertaining. I'm even less than ordinary in some of these areas. I do these things anyway out of necessity or for the pure joy of doing them.

In the book of Exodus, we read about God using ordinary people, Moses and Aaron, to perform wonders.

Which of our ordinary talents might we use to perform wonders, to bless others, or simply to improve ourselves and our environment?

Cheesebox Accounting

For most of my life I have used a simple system for keeping a running record of my financial matters. It's called cheese box accounting. I use one cheese box for receipts for supplies and expenses for my craft business. They are automatically in chronological order because I put them in the back of the box as soon as I get them. Another cheese box contains the receipts for income from my crafts. There is no accounts payable box because I write a check for everything when I buy it.

Then there's the cheese box for household bills. It's labeled by weeks and I put the bills in the section for the week before it's due. If a bill is urgent I stand it on its end so I will remember to pay it first. If a bill is wider than a cheese box, it doesn't deserve to be paid. It goes in the garbage can.

When I get some money from my regular job, I give some to God (church or charity) first. God has promised to provide for our needs if we do that. Of course, sometimes God and I disagree as to the definition of needs so my checkbook may be a mess. But if it doesn't balance, or if there isn't enough money to pay everything right away, I can say, "It's God's fault. He wanted His money first."

After I pay God, I take out grocery money, then I go to the "bills" cheese box. I pay the standing-up bills first, then work my way through the weeks until the money is gone. The paid bills go in the "bills paid" cheese box, of course. The system works for me.

At the end of the year, I sit down with my cheese boxes and total up everything by months. I make 12 income entries and 12 expense entries in my little two-column cash book, subtract, and there's my profit for the year. All of this is accomplished in about two hours with no help from a computer which would produce tables A through M and spit out 15 pages of business analysis.

About once a year, usually sometime close to the dreaded IRS deadline of April 15, I determine to get control of my budget and finances. I really do try. One year I even went so far as to invest in an elaborate eight-column accounting book. I labeled the columns and started making entries every time I bought supplies or sold an item. By the time I remembered where I put the accounting book, found a pen, and decided where to post the item, I had wasted 15 minutes of time. That was not an efficient use of my time and I still had to use a cheese box for storing my receipts. I was duplicating my work and causing myself frequent and unnecessary frustration. I started to snap at my son and kick the dog. I don't typically kick dogs. I decided that organization is not worth a nervous breakdown so I threw the accounting book away and went back to my cheese boxes.

If the IRS ever audits me, they'll just have to nibble their way through my cheese boxes. Maybe in the process, they will learn something about efficient use of time, simplicity of operation, prioritizing, frugality, and paper reduction.

Driving Cadillac Style–NOT

My car was having one of its stubborn streaks and wanted some attention from its favorite mechanic. In the meantime, I had to find transportation for the forty-mile trip to my job.

Since I work nights, my son graciously offered me the use of his 1980 Impala because he would need it only during the day. I was a bit dubious about driving a somewhat rusty vehicle with something hanging kind of low underneath, but I hated to turn down his generosity and didn't have another option available.

Steve hovered over me as I checked out what I needed to know before I started out on my adventure.

"It has a good motor in it, Mom, and it runs really good once you get it started. Getting it started is the tricky part. It's tricky because there's a clothespin on the carburetor. So you have to keep tapping the gas pedal until you get the air out of the gas line. Just gently, tap, tap, tap, or you'll flood it. But it runs real good after you get it started."

"Okay. Let me practice while you watch in case I don't do it right."

The seat was adjusted to make room for a 6'2" body so I wanted to push it ahead to accommodate my 5'6" stature. I finally found a lever of sorts and jerked it ahead. The driver's side of the seat moved ahead nicely, but the passenger half of the wide seat stayed where it was. Oh, well. A seat at a 30 degree angle wouldn't bother my driving.

"Why is this oil pressure gauge hanging down here by my feet?"

"I guess a couple of screws fell out."

"So do I need to lean down and look at it once in awhile?"

"No, Mom. You don't need to worry about that. It doesn't use any oil."

He continued his instructions. "The left-turn signal works, but it doesn't go off after you've turned. You have to remember to turn it off."

"No problem, Steve. I learned how to drive when I had to stick my arm out of the window to signal a turn. I can handle a partially-functioning turn signal."

"It kind of looks like rain," I observed. "What do I need to know about the windshield wipers?"

"You turn them on here. They work just fine, but you have to turn them off exactly where you want them to stop because they don't go down by themselves."

"I see the radio speakers are on the floor. Sometimes I like music while I'm driving. Does your radio work?"

"The tape player works better. All you get from the radio is a blast of static."

"And another thing. Try to park where you won't have to back up. I can back it up, but you might have some trouble with reverse. It's kind of tricky."

I assured him that the parking lot at work is large enough so I would be able to park facing home. He wouldn't have to worry about that.

"It's a little on the warm side tonight. Does your air-conditioner work?"

"It kind of works but you'll probably need to roll the window down a little."

"One last thing. Whatever you do, don't try to open the door on the passenger side. If you get it open, it won't stay shut again and might fly open while you're going around a curve. Don't worry about it, though. I have it locked."

"So what you're telling me is that if I decide to be foolish enough to pick up a hitchhiker, he wouldn't be able to get in?"

"Mom, a hitchhiker wouldn't be foolish enough to accept a ride in this car. He'd wait for a better offer."

"Thanks, Steve. I feel better now."

Hair

Next to, "Clean your room, it looks like a pigsty," the most common request parents make of their children is probably, "Get a haircut," although in the case of head shaving, it might be, "Please let it grow out. Soon."

I would imagine that such discussions have gone on since the beginning of humankind and that they will continue as long as people have children.

In the seventies, the symbol of teenage rebellion was blue jeans with holes in the knees and hems that were long enough to walk on. It didn't matter what kind of shirt was worn with the jeans because the waist-length straight hair covered it. Unisex clothes. Unisex hair. That gave parents and teenagers at least three years of intense debate.

The sixties brought such styles as beehives and other variations of upswept hairdos that required backcombing. After each strand was ratted or teased it was saturated with hairspray, the stiffer the better. This style could not be combed or washed easily, so often stayed put for a week or ten days in its original state without combing or washing.

The rage of the fifties was the crew cut until it was pushed aside to make room for the Elvis bangs, sideburns and ducktails. Huge brush rollers gave body to pageboys but sleeping on them at night was uncomfortable to say the least.

I remember my mother forming finger waves in her hair and securing them in place with clamps and making pincurls which when combed out left kinks where the bobby pins had been. Her grandchildren remember her wearing pink sponge rollers in her hair after her Saturday shampoo.

Sometimes I got upset over my children's hair, but I tried to remember some of my own not-so-wonderful experiences and experiments with hair.

My Aunt Esther loved home permanents. She loved to have someone put one in her hair and she loved to give my mother, sisters, and me home permanents. It was an all-day job to do that many heads of hair, especially when we had long hair. Unfortunately, I had naturally curly hair, so I could have gotten by with a neat, short, natural hair style, but she didn't want me to be left out. If one of us got something, we'd all better get it.

I'll never forget the time she put 99 little rollers in my hair. What a fashion statement that was! Nothing short of a curry comb would have taken the snarls out of that pile of tresses after a day in the Dakota wind.

When I was in high school, our school colors were green and gold, so some of us on the girls basketball team decided to show some real school spirit by dyeing one side of our hair green and the other side gold. The green food coloring worked great on one side but the yellow for the other side didn't show. So we tried butter coloring which was oily and didn't really work. During the home game, my friend played so hard she worked up a sweat and the greasy butter coloring ran down her face and dripped onto her uniform. Not real attractive.

So whenever I start to get judgmental about current fads and get on my soapbox about the "ridiculous hairstyles of the young people nowadays" I just remind myself to get out the old photograph albums and take a short walk down memory lane.

What's for Potluck?

Everyone loves a church potluck. Well, almost everyone. It gives people who are into cooking a chance to exhibit their talents and share their favorite foods with others. It gives those who hate to cook a chance to eat something tasty without having to plan and prepare a whole meal.

One church is extremely organized in its potlucks and assigns hot dishes to those whose last names begin with A-H, desserts to those with I-O, etc. so that a balance will be assured. Another church just says potluck. Only once in twenty years did they have one hotdish and 30 desserts. Occasionally there will be seven bean casseroles, but nobody complains. The beans all taste different and almost everybody likes beans.

It's always interesting to see the variety of foods which people consider to be their best efforts. There might be German kuchen or sauerkraut with deer sausage, Irish stew, Norwegian lefse, and English scones. During the garden season there will be bowls of cucumbers lathered in cream and huge plates of sliced tomatoes. The pot full of strong coffee sits at its usual place at the end of the table unless the persons in charge get creative and move it to another table in which case we are sure to hear, "Why is the coffee pot on this table? We've never done it this way before."

Once in awhile somebody has to take an almost-full casserole home with them. It's not that the casserole isn't good, it's just that it looked pale in comparison to the Oriental stir fry with sweet and sour sauce on a bed of long-grained rice.

Kids look over the array of marvelous salads and main dishes made with exotic and expensive ingredients and opt for a catsup-and-mustard-smothered hotdog on a bun which they wolf down in five minutes so they can go out and play football in the church parking lot.

The ultimate compliment at a potluck is to have three people ask for the recipe. The recipe is graciously given with the knowledge that at the next potluck, there will be three different versions of that recipe on the table.

Almost always, somebody spills something. The worst is the grape Kool-aid on the light-colored carpet. Scolding parent, beware. You may be the one who spills the salsa on the newly-purchased white linen tablecloth.

Church potlucks are a time for food, fellowship and fun. They are the stuff of which memories are made and friendships are nourished. As long as we are trusting enough to take a chance on something someone else has cooked, civilization survives.

The County Fair

The County Fair was the highlight of the summer for the Schmidt family. It was the culmination of a year of hard work on 4-H projects and the last chance to have some fun with friends before school started.

Exhibits for gardening projects were always a frustration. Hayley and Dan fought over the biggest pumpkin and picked three rows of green beans to find ten that were of uniform size and shape. The carrot row looked as if moles had been at work. Clem pretended nonchalance while Dan and Haley scrambled to get five perfect red tomatoes then he went down the row and picked five perfect, solid green tomatoes. He remembered that last year the purple ribbon tomatoes were green. Cora remembered the hassle of garden projects and didn't enroll in gardening.

Dad and the boys loaded Dan's Red Angus steer and Clem's Yorkshire hog into the horse trailer and put Dan's bundle of ten-foot hybrid field corn and Clem's sunflowers in the pickup. Clem said, "Dan, don't forget your currycomb like you did last year. And be sure you have enough money for carnival rides so you don't have to borrow from me again."

Mama and the girls loaded the van to the windows with garden produce, sewing projects, canned vegetables, baked goods, and demonstration posters.

Cora's vest, blouse, and skirt outfit had been finished at the end of June. She had followed the directions meticulously and her stitches were perfect. She knew she would get the purple ribbon on her project and was already planning what she might do with the premium money. She had spent hours throughout the year on her child care scrapbook and she had taken four 36-exposure rolls of film to get that spectacular Dakota sunset in fiery oranges and pinks. The cream-colored mat contrasted with the vibrant colors in the photo and Cora thought that the rustic frame made from scraps in Dad's workshop gave it exactly the country accent it needed.

On the way to town, Hayley propped her floral arrangement between her feet to keep the water from spilling. She thought, "My glads are pretty, but the bachelor's buttons look kind of sick. Oh, well, my chickens will get a blue ribbon again this year."

The hens squawked and pecked from their wire cage in the seat beside her while she finished hemming her blue calico skirt. She hoped the judge wouldn't notice that she hadn't put the interfacing in the waistband. That took too much time and she had more interesting things to do than to pay attention to all those silly details.

Mama was glad she had stayed up until two a.m. the night before to finish the border on her Stunning Stars quilt in shades of green and mauve. It was sure to get the People's Choice Award in the quilt display. She had baked a 7-grain bread to exhibit in open class. Last year her frosted cinnamon twist had brought the highest bid at the bread sale.

She smiled as she drove and said, "Girls, when you grow up and have families of your own, you will remember these days as the best days of your lives. I hope you pass these country traditions on to your children."

Cora and Hayley looked at each other and rolled their eyes.

Mama just kept on smiling as she whistled a happy tune.

Dieting - An American Paradox

She's tall, perhaps 5'10", weighs 110 pounds, wears a size three, has long blonde hair and sultry green eyes, a chest measurement of 40 inches and a waist of 23.

Look around, guys. Have you seen someone like that lately except in your dreams or mincing across your television screen? Chances are slim to none that you will find her in the real world yet she's the one most guys covet and many gals try to emulate.

We look at one of the plethora of catalogs that fill our mailboxes and can't help but see the irony in the one called Pretty Plus with perfect size 10's modeling size 24 clothes. What a let-down for the gullible woman who orders the wild red print on page 26 with the catalog image in her mind.

So American women are obsessed with dieting. They will try any fad that comes along if it promises to shape them into their mental perception of perfection. Most diets work for awhile, but a steady diet of grapefruit, celery and carrot sticks gets tiresome and depressing and the dieter is right back to old eating habits again. The see-saw dieter diets, loses a little weight, eats, gains weight, feels guilty, goes on another diet, loses some weight again but not enough quickly enough, gets discouraged and eats more, gains more, has more guilt, and tries yet another diet.

We want a quick-fix to weight problems. Maybe we can take a pill or drink a glass of something that tastes good but is guaranteed to absorb the bad stuff or get it out of our systems if we happen to eat the wrong foods that we love so much. We are willing to take a prescription drug no matter how many side effects the doctor or pharmacist warns us we might suffer. Maybe we can lose that weight while sleeping or without exercising which makes the ads all the more appealing.

While all of that craziness is going on, we are bombarded with commercials for food. A pizzeria offers an extra-large with four cheeses for the price of a medium. Super Burger begs us to come in and get their maxi-half-pounder with a triple order of fries and a 22-ounce drink. Restaurants advertise their taco salad in a bread bowl big enough for three people. We go to church potlucks and everything looks so good that we sample a bit of everything. We have our morning coffee break. While we hold our cup of coffee in our right hand, we need something for the left hand to do, so we have a monster cookie or a caramel roll that covers a dinner plate.

We feel obligated to eat everything on our plates. It's what Mamas teach us to do. Mama loves us so she cooks a big kettle of dumplings for us. If we love her, we will eat a generous portion and ask for a second helping. When we can't eat everything on our plates and Mama says, "Eat! Starving children in Africa would be happy to have your leftovers," she is probably right. Perhaps we should eat less so others can have something.

We can't pick up a newspaper or magazine without reading an article about the latest findings in nutrition. These articles tell us which foods will maintain healthy bones, skin, muscles, teeth, and various other body parts. This information can be useful and informative. These articles also tell us which foods are dangerous to our health and well-being. Isn't it amazing that for all of the foods that can harm us our life-expectancy keeps going up?

In elementary school we were taught that we should eat a balanced diet of the basic food groups which are fruits and vegetables, meat and other proteins, grain products, and dairy foods. We were taught to eat moderate portions of a variety of foods from each group.

Perhaps we need to go back to the basics.

Exercise - Who, Me?

My last article was about dieting. Sad to say, we can hardly talk about dieting without following up with dialogue on exercising, so I'll do my best to address that topic.

Experts tell us that if we lose weight, we must concurrently exercise to tone up the muscles and the skin to eliminate flab. They also tell us that exercising will help to reduce the occurrence of osteoporosis. Since flab is not a pretty-sounding concept and I can't picture myself losing bone mass, I will exercise.

I'll start with a low-impact video featuring a lithe blond named Bambi, Trixie who is a stunning brunette, and Rambo, whose name speaks for itself. Just walking across the living room to insert the tape into the VCR makes me tired enough to need to sit down with a cup of hot green tea and relax for a few minutes.

I finish my tea, hit the VCR play button and watch intently as Bambi appears in her little black leotard, full of enthusiasm and ready to demonstrate contortions beyond comprehension.

"Bend at the waist, hands flat on the floor, and hold for a count of five," she coaches. "Don't worry if you can't touch the floor, just bend as far as you can. You'll work up to it. Watch Trixie if you have trouble doing the exercises. She's doing the easy version."

I carry on a running commentary in response to the absurdities I hear from the pretty people on the screen.

"Sure, she should do the easy stuff. She has abs as flat as an ironing board and looks like she's been in fitness training since the day she was born."

"Now let's do the squats. When you bend, don't let your knees extend past your toes. Pretend like you're sitting on a chair then slowly get off the chair."

"So give me a chair.

"Remember if you can't go down as far as I do, watch Trixie. Move as far as you can."

"It's not the going down that's hard. It's the getting back up again."

"Now grasp your left ankle with your hands."

"And do what with my right leg? You've got to be kidding."

"Sit on the floor, feet apart, and touch your knee with your forehead."

"So tell Trixie to put a spare tire around her middle and see how far she can lean over."

Bambi continues her annoying chatter. "Don't give up. This session is only eight minutes long. We're half way there. Keep breathing."

"What are my options?"

"Squat, kick left, squat, kick right. When it burns, go for it. That's when it counts. You're doing great."

"Yah, right. I'm lying on my back in the middle of the floor gasping for air. How much greater can I be?"

"In eight minutes, we've worked every muscle in the lower body. Now Rambo will show us what to do for the upper body. Remember this section takes only eight minutes. You can do it."

Rambo, muscles bulging, takes his turn at giving directions and demonstrations. "Pick up your weights. I'm using 50 pounds, but start out

32

with whatever you are comfortable with. Bambi is using fifteen pounds, Trixie, ten."

"Sorry, Rambo. Three-pound weights or a tomato-soup can is about all I can handle."

"Out to the side, even with the shoulder and down. Up, down, up, down."

"Owwwie, owwwie."

"Curl in front of your chest, lift over your head, straight up, down to your chest again, and curl down to your side."

"I think I hurt myself. Call 911."

Then Trixie takes her turn at imparting important information. "Remember, after exercising it's important to cool down. Don't skip this eight-minute cool-down section."

"Of course not, Trixie. This is the part I'm good at."

"Roll your shoulders up and forward as far as you can, hold, then reverse them, up and back. Hold. Again. You're doing great. Drop your head slowly forward and let it rest there for the count of ten."

"One... two..... three.......zzzzzzzzzzzz."

Sadie Saves Again

Sadie is a sporadic rebater. Most of the time she simply can't be bothered with coupon clipping and label snipping. But once in awhile she goes into her bargain hunting mode and tells herself that she really ought to be more careful with the family budget and shop more wisely.

So last week when Homer picked up the Sunday paper he found it riddled with oblong-shaped holes and said, "Kids, prepare yourselves for some surprises. Your mother is on a bargain binge again!"

Sadie clipped and cut and sorted. She dragged out her envelopes and cheeseboxes and coupon organizers full of coupons and rebate forms, some still usable, dozens outdated. She filled the wastebasket three times, and sorted all the possibilities into neat little stacks to correspond with the merchandise aisles at the grocery store. She became organization personified as she made her lists for the dairy aisle, the canned goods aisles and on throughout the store. This was exciting and Sadie lost track of time as she contemplated the savings she was going to rack up at the check-out counter.

On Monday at SuperShop Sadie became a militant shopper as she whipped her cart up one aisle and down another, mercilessly cutting in front of the slow-moving carts, grabbing the last pair of the two-for-the-price-of-one chicken patties before Grandma Smith got them and leaving tread marks on the floor in front of the popcorn display.

She was on a mission and had no consideration at all for other shoppers. By the time she was ready to check out, she had filled three carts. She nearly passed out right on the spot when the clerk told her the total and it was $80 over her monthly grocery budget. "Oh, well," she thought, "just think of all the money I've saved. I can hardly wait to get home to figure out my savings."

Her kids met her at the door to help her carry in the surprises and check to see if there was anything for them. Her son said, "Mom, why did you buy Baby Dipes? We haven't had a baby in the house for years. Decaslim? Mom, if you lose any more weight, you'll blow away in the wind. What's this pain-killer for? I can't even pronounce it. Do you have a headache? An empty candy bar wrapper? Mom, how could you?"

Sadie said, "I did get a little carried away, didn't I? But you never know when someone with a baby might be visiting and needs an extra diaper. Maybe my sister can use the Decaslim and you never know when you might get a headache. It's good to be prepared. And the candy bar? I had only one coupon for a free Chocomint Delight. I ate it on the way home so you kids wouldn't fight over it. Besides, sugar is bad for your teeth."

Her daughter said, "This supply of coffee filters will last until your great-grandchildren arrive."

Sadie said, "Hush, child. They were a steal at buy-two-get-one-free."

There was no sleep for Sadie. At 1 a.m. she was still scraping labels off the spaghetti and ripping the toilet paper apart. Trying to figure out how to fill out the rebates, which UPC's and cash register receipts to use, and which prices to circle was indeed giving Sadie a headache and she tried to pry the child-proof cap off the unpronounceable pain killer. The four 100-ounce plastic jugs of laundry soap were soaking in a tub full of hot water to loosen the labels with the UPC's. The corn flakes crunched underfoot because the box was minus its bottom and the liner had been punctured accidentally. The cans without their labels were lined up neatly on the cupboard shelves and the wrapperless summer sausage was drying out in the refrigerator.

Sadie muttered, "I hope my family appreciates how hard I'm working to save money and balance the budget," as she cut her hand on a tin can lid while trying to retrieve the apple bag twisty from the bottom of the 30-gallon garbage bag.

When Sadie totaled her rebates, added her coupon savings, subtracted the postage, figured her time at minimum wage, and deducted her mileage she had saved a grand total of $13.29. She didn't know whether to laugh or cry.

She said to herself (nobody else was awake to listen), "I'm going back to nature. Let me plant my garden, milk a cow, butcher a chicken, grind some wheat. I'll serve anything that doesn't have a UPC, offer a rebate form, or need a coupon.

The Paper Boy

Eddy begged to have a paper route. He had grandiose plans of buying video games and saving enough money for an impressive pickup truck.

His parents thought a paper route would be good for Eddy. It would teach him responsibility and give him an opportunity to earn some spending money and some to put away for college. He would learn how to run a business and deal with people.

They explained to him that he was making a commitment, that he would have to get up early every morning whether he felt like it or not. They had him get out the calculator and do a little math. They reminded him that sometimes he would be short papers or someone would take his papers from the drop-off point and he would have to try to find a place to buy replacements. They told him that sometimes people don't pay the paper boy, or their checks bounce, or they move away owing for two months of deliveries.

"That's the real world, Son," they told him.

He was not to be deterred.

He signed up to deliver 40 dailies and 60 Sundays. He made his deliveries faithfully every morning and kept soliciting new customers. It was easy for him to put the dailies into his backpack and walk the route or ride his bike, but on Sunday morning the papers were so thick and heavy that it required some team work. Sometimes Eddy could get his little brother to help him if he gave him a dollar or let him ride the big bike. Mother usually volunteered to help insert the various Sunday flyers, circulars, and ads. If it was really cold, Mother or Dad would volunteer to drive him around the route. Otherwise he had to make at least six trips and they'd never get the papers delivered in time to go to church.

At one time, paper boys got a break on Christmas Day, but when Eddy got a route, he had to deliver the special edition on Christmas morning, the big special edition with all of the after-Christmas sales circulars.

One morning there was a blizzard. The snow was blowing so that they couldn't see the house across the street. There was no possibility of mail or papers arriving and no one was going anywhere so the whole family could have slept a little later than usual. Helga called threatening to cancel her subscription because the paper boy forgot to deliver her paper. Mother had worked late the night before and she was not a happy camper.

Helga also called the day that there were no coupon inserts in her paper. She said, "I want my coupons. What did you do with my coupons? The only reason I get the Sunday paper is for the coupons."

She didn't believe Eddy when he told her there were none that day.

Edith lived in an old house hidden behind tall bushes in a scary part of town. When Eddy had to deliver her paper before the sun came up in the winter, she left the porch light on for him so it wasn't quite so scary. He was surprised and excited when he found an envelope with a five-dollar bill in it taped to the storm door on his birthday. He wondered how she knew it was his birthday.

Eddy always allowed at least an extra five minutes to talk to Grandpa Schwartz. Grandpa sat by his living room window and watched for his paper. He was lonely and Eddy knew what to say to cheer him up and make him smile.

After Dad took the tenth phone call from upset customers on the rainy morning when the papers got wet at the drop-off point behind the post-office because they hadn't been wrapped in plastic, he said, "Eddy, when you grow up, I hope you have a dozen children and they ALL have paper routes!"

Eddy said, "I hope so, too, Dad. This is really fun."

It's a Guy Thing

You can tell without looking whether a man or a woman pulls into your driveway.

The guy who drives in makes all the noise he can. Before he turns the key in the ignition, he revs the motor. Vrrrrmmmm. Vrrrrmmmm. He gets out, raises the hood, takes a good long look at all those parts and pieces moving, slams the hood down and then turns the motor off. Next, he takes a stroll around the vehicle and kicks at a tire or two.

A woman simply stops the car, turns off the motor, and quietly shuts her door. She can probably sneak in without you hearing her.

A woman slows gradually when approaching an intersection with a red light. A guy goes full speed until he's right at the crosswalk then slams on the brake. And when the light turns to green, the woman again rolls gently into motion. The guy guns the motor to get ahead of the car beside him.

In the winter time after a blizzard, a woman will wait for the snowplow to go through. A guy will tool around to see how much snow he can plow. If someone says to him, "You'll never make it through this drift," his stock phrase is, "Sure I can. I have 4-wheel drive." Never mind that the snow bank is higher than the truck.

If a woman tries to pass an 18-wheeler on an Interstate, the truck driver seems to think it would be an insult to his manhood to let her go around him. A woman will let everything pass her as she crawls along enjoying the scenery.

If something goes wrong with a motor, a guy will try to fix it himself even if he hasn't a clue as to what's wrong. He will replace four different parts and spend twenty-five hours trying to figure out how to make it run before he gives up and has it towed into the shop. A woman will call a mechanic the minute it dies and have the car out and running in two hours with no frustration on her part.

Last week I got to thinking maybe I've been missing something with my cautious driving habits. I got on Interstate and passed everything on the road, weaving in and out of traffic like I was late for a wedding. I didn't eat anybody's exhaust.

When I got into town and hit a red light I slammed on the brakes at the last split second. When the light turned green, I was half-way down the block before the 4 x 4 beside me got into the intersection.

I drove into my driveway, revved the motor, vrrrrmmmm, vrrrrmmmm, got out and lifted the hood to see if everything was still turning. I turned the motor off then walked around the car and kicked the right rear tire.

Hey, that was kind of fun. Maybe I'll try it again sometime.

My Daughter, the Waitress

...and what does *your* daugher do, Elaine?"

The question comes up often when people are discussing the accomplishments of their adult children.

"My daugher's a waitress."

"Oh."

"Connie enjoys being a waitress. She loves to meet people and she's very good at her job."

"Oh. Well, it's nice to enjoy your work," and the conversation moves on quickly to other topics.

In Acts 6:2-4 we read, "It is not right that we (the disciples) should give up preaching the word of God to serve tables. Therefore, brethren, pick out from among you seven men of good repute, full of the Spirit and of wisdom, whom we may appoint to this duty. But we will devote ourselves to prayer and to the ministry of the word."

Does anyone ever think of a waitress as being filled with the Spirit and of wisdom, that she has intellectual capacity? Yet, think of how much wisdom is required to deal with people at their basic-needs level. Customers are often tired, impatient, demanding. They may be upset, upset over their food which the waitress didn't cook, or upset over the prices, which she didn't set, or upset over mix-ups in reservations which she didn't make. The only visible person the customer has for registering a complaint is— the waitress. She *is* the business as the public sees it, and very often she's the one who gets the least respect from customers as well as management.

Connie has worked under all kinds of managers. She's had managers who treat everyone fairly and truly care about their customers and employees. She's had managers who don't know how to handle people.

One of them gave the best shifts and most hours to any waitress who welcomed his sexual advances. Connie worked a lot of breakfast shifts for him. Nobody tips for breakfast.

One job that Connie had paid $2.01 per hour because employers are expecting that a waitress receives 15 percent of ticket sales in tips. However, a lot of people don't tip that much. Then in addition to that, Congress passed the allocated tip law. I'm still trying to figure out exactly how that works. At the end of the shift the waitress is allocated a percentage of her total ticket sales which is reported as earned income whether she receives tips or not. Social Security and federal withholding taxes on this reported income are deducted from her paycheck.

Connie has learned to make jokes about her occupation. When asked what she does for a living, she says, "I'm a food technician, specializing in sales."

She loves people, enjoys serving, and can start a conversation with anyone. She has the special gift of being able to use a joke or a kind word to handle awkward situations or unhappy customers.

One chilly winter night a young man came into her section. He was feeling miserable with a terrible cold. Connie went out to the kitchen and made him a cup of hot tea with honey and lemon. As she served him she said, "Anybody who feels like you do needs this. Compliments of your waitress." He was surprised, to be sure.

Connie tells of the young father who brought his five small daughters in for pizza. They all sat with hands under the table until she served them. They all smiled and said, "Thank you," when she brought their milk. She said, "Sir, I would like to compliment you."

"Why?"

"You have taught your children well."

He smiled and said, "Thank you."

What a contrast to the father who brought his teenage daughters in for supper. He pinched her, made snide remarks and treated her most disrespectfully. She was astonished when she found a very large tip on her table after they left, but was appalled at the lesson which that father was teaching his daughters—that it's acceptable to abuse people in serving positions as long as they get paid for it.

Waitressing is extemely stressful in addition to being physically demanding, so I rejoice with my daugher that she has chosen another occupation as well. But I will never respect her more than I have for being "just a waitress," er, excuse me, a food technician, specializing in sales.

The Quiet Ones

The quiet people are hardly noticed in a world where people are screaming for attention, shouting their opinions and protesting infringements upon their rights. Those who are aggressive and vocal get publicity and recognition.

Let's look for some of these quiet people in our circle of acquaintances.

She's the invisible child who sits quietly in the classroom. Since she never speaks out nor draws attention to herself, she is considered a "good child." She always knows the answers to the teacher's questions, or has a good idea or an interesting opinion but she's too introverted to raise her hand. Since she doesn't volunteer, nobody asks her. She may even be considered "slow."

She's the one who sees the hurt in your eyes when you don't make the team and softly touches your shoulder. Without a word, you know she cares and understands.

He's the good-looking boy with the big brown eyes who sits in study hall behind the cute little blond. He would like to ask her to the prom but he's too shy. Since he never gets up the courage to talk to her, she thinks he's not interested and ignores him.

She's the lady in the church kitchen washing dishes and cleaning up the mess. When no one is looking, she puts food in the basket for the food pantry and puts a little extra money in the plate for the youth group's camping trip. When someone is in the hospital, her presence beside the bed is comforting and her prayers are reassuring.

He's the man who sits in the back row at the town meeting. He's an intelligent man but hesitates to speak out with his ideas for city planning. Since he doesn't say anything, he isn't chosen for the planning committee, even though he would be capable and willing to work if someone would ask him to help.

She's the grandmother who takes the time to walk along the river with her grandson. She walks slowly so they can look for baby frogs in the grass. She shows him how to make a whistle from a tall blade of grass. They talk about where the river runs, where the sun sleeps at night and what the wind is whispering about.

We all know some of these quiet people. Sometimes they are the best friends we ever have.

My Special Grandpa

The rain pounded on the roof as I tried to sleep the night after Grandpa's funeral.

I cried because of the loss of a very special person in my life and I cried because the baby stirring within me would never know my Grandpa.

The world would certainly be a better place if every child in the world could have a Grandpa like mine, a Grandpa who loved and accepted not only his own grandchildren, but all the children he knew.

When my Grandpa told a story, he made it so funny and so real that the only way we knew whether it was true or not was to watch for the twinkle in his eye. Reading and reciting were major pastimes when he was growing up and he would entertain us by the hour with our special requests for *Casey at the Bat* or *Abou Ben Adhem*.

I wish I had listened more closely to the real stories he told of his days of hard physical work, days of homesteading and logging in the Black Hills, days of farming in North Dakota, stories about my Dad and his brothers and sisters. There are so many questions I'd like to ask him now, and experiences I'd like to hear about.

When my sisters and I spent part of our summer vacation with Grandpa, we waded in the creek while he hoed the corn on his little farm. I can still picture him in my mind, wearing his sweat-stained tan work shirt, the tan khaki pants rolled up to keep the dirt out of his cuffs, the sturdy brown laced work boots, his worn straw hat atop the red hair streaked with gray.

When we sang "Three Little Sisters" or "Mocking Bird Hill" he told us it was pretty and asked us to sing some more even though we couldn't carry a tune in a bushel basket. The cribbage board, playing cards, and dominoes were always in the top drawer of the buffet and with very little coaxing, we could challenge him to a game at the kitchen table.

No matter what we were playing, Grandpa amazed me by doing the numbers in his head when I had to have paper and pencil to figure things out and keep track of the scores.

Grandpa never recovered financially from losses during the Great Depression. When he died, he had only a hundred dollars to his name, but he left his grandchildren a million-dollar legacy of love, humor, integrity, and loyal commitment to his family and friends.

Sometimes I wish I could say to him one more time, "Grandpa, will you tell me a story about the olden days?"

I would listen more carefully.

A Worry for All Ages

When John was young, he thought that when he reached middle age, whatever that might be, he would have it made. Money in the bank, children self-sufficient. Yes, life would be on cruise. He could relax a little with nothing more to worry about.

But as he thought about his life, he realized that every age has its problems and no one is immune to troubles, concerns, and worries.

When he was six months old, he worried, "Will someone come to hold me and feed me and talk to me? How long will it be before someone notices I need to be taken care of?"

At age three as he tried to sleep in the scary darkness of his room his imagination ran wild. "There's a tiger under my bed and an alligator in my closet. Who will come to protect me?"

Starting school brought even bigger worries. "Can I cross the street by myself? Will I find a friend? What if I can't get to the bathroom in time? Will I ever get a star for writing my numbers? Maybe I can't color inside the lines."

Fifth grade didn't get any easier. "Will I pass the math test? Can I figure out what the big words mean? What will I do if I get valentines from girls? Whose team can I be on at recess? Why do I have to be the smallest one in my class?"

The year he started junior high was the worst. "Why do the big kids want to beat us up? What if a girl likes me? What if no girl ever likes me? Will I find a good friend? Why haven't I started a growth spurt yet?"

His senior year was the toughest. "I have zits on my forehead just in time for the prom. What do I want to be when I grow up? Do I have to grow up? I can't wait to get out of here. But where will I go when I get out of here?"

When he was 25 he thought about his responsibilities as an adult. "Will I be a good husband? What if I can't provide for my children? Will I always have to work at a job I don't like? Should I rent an apartment or should I invest in a house? How much should I pay for a vehicle?"

When John's friends helped him celebrate his 50th birthday, he tried to enjoy the party and see the humor of it all. He didn't tell anyone his thoughts. "I've lived half a century. Have I really made a difference to anyone in the world? Have I made enough money, bought enough stuff? And if I have, why am I still not contented? What else does God want me to do with my life? Is there something more, or is this it?"

Most people look forward to their retirement, but at age 65 John thought, "Can I live on Social Security? Somehow I was never able to save enough or invest enough to live on in my old age. Will I be healthy enough to keep on working? Will my employer let me go and hire a younger person?"

At the age of 83, John had a heart attack. He asked, " Could I manage in an assisted-living apartment? Should I sell my house or keep it in case I'm able to go back to it? I don't want to be a burden to my children."

When he was 95 and in the nursing home he thought, "Will someone come to hold me and feed me and talk to me? When will someone notice I need to be taken care of?"

The Wonder of a Baby

As a mother holds her newborn baby for the first time there is this moment only. Time stands still as she examines the baby and marvels at how perfect and how tiny are the 10 toes and 10 specks of fingernails. She puts her finger in the baby's hand and feels it tighten into a fist as if making an attempt to communicate for the first time. She thinks, "Are these legs normal? They look too small and too crooked. She has ears like Grandpa and a button nose like Aunt Jen. Where's her neck? I wonder if the eyes will be blue or if they will get darker."

There are the fears.

"What if I don't wake up when she cries during the night? What if I'm not a good mother? How will I know if she's sick or just fussy? What if I can't provide adequately for her needs? What if I'm inadequate to the task of nurturing, loving, training, teaching, disciplining and being a good example?"

There are musings of the possibilities.

"Will she have a sense of humor or will she have a serious, contemplative nature?

Will she be a ray of sunshine on a cloudy day or will she be a storm cloud moving in on a sunny day?

Will she have her mother's aggressive disposition or will she be gentle and calm like her father?

Will the world be kind to her or will she be short-changed because she's a woman?

Will she contribute in a positive way to make the world a better place or will she contribute to the problems of the world?

Will she be the person to find a cure for cancer or AIDS, or will she be a creative and carefree spirit?

Will she be the first woman president or will she marry a farmer and work beside him in the field?

Will she use the talents and abilities that God has given her to carry out the plan that He has created her to fulfill or will she deny His existence and His importance in her life?"

Parenthood holds many surprises. But as a mother holds and gently rocks her newborn baby, her mind tends to focus on the positive possibilities and she cherishes the dreams and holds the hopes in her heart. Never at any other time in her life does she feel so profoundly the wonder and awe of God's creation.

Let Children Be Children

Not long ago I was visiting with a young mother who was complaining because she had helped her first-grader with three hours of homework the night before.

I thought, "Three hours of homework for a first-grader? Unbelievable! I didn't have homework until I was in high school and I learned more than I needed to know."

Children have to sit still in school for seven hours and that doesn't include long bus rides for many of them. When do they get time for physical activities?

They need to climb a tree, ride a bicycle, or skip rope. They need time to talk to their parents, play with brothers, sisters, or friends. They need time to dream, to pretend, to try out their own ideas. They need time to look at the clouds and run barefoot in the new green grass. They need time to make things without worrying about whether they are doing it right or putting the right answer in the blank. Play is a child's work. Play is the child's way of learning about the environment and how to get along with other people.

Formal education is important, of course, but it isn't the only form of education. People used to quit school after eighth grade and many of them have lived happy, prosperous lives. Then high-school graduation became the norm. That was a good thing. Kindergarten also is a good thing. It prepares children for first grade.

Now we have pre-school and head start to prepare them for kindergarten and day care centers are expected to provide structured days to prepare children for pre-school.

All of this, yet we read report after report about how our schools are failing.

Perhaps society is expecting more from the schools than they are able to do. If that is true, then what changes should be made?

Another area of concern in children's education is television, the teacher with whom they spend the most time outside of school. Children are bombarded with adult ideas, overexposed to violence and stupidity, and encouraged to emulate role models with immoral lifestyles.

The first comment we hear if we complain about the programs is that we can turn it off. Indeed we should turn it off on a regular basis. But even if we are in the middle of a really decent show, commercials and program previews are shown and the trash is right there before we have a chance to flick the remote.

In Corrie Ten Boom's book *The Hiding Place* she wrote about the time when she was very young and she and her father were waiting for a train. She said to her father, "What is sex sin?"

Her father said, "Corrie, can you pick up my suitcase?"

She tried and tried, but it was too heavy for her. Her father told her she was too young to lift the suitcase and she was too young to know about sex sin.

Maybe this enlightened generation thinks he handled the question badly. I think it was wise.

He wanted his children to be children.

Living Country Style

Recently I watched some reruns of black-and-white features of Elvis Presley. One of the saddest things he said was, "I get lonesome right in the middle of a crowd."

How tragic to have talent, charisma, money, and fame and yet feel alone!

That remark stuck with me and I thought about my own life, and how I have never felt lonely even when I'm alone. I think my upbringing has had something to do with that.

I grew up on a ranch west of Fort Pierre. We often joked that we lived thirty miles from nowhere in every direction. Our ranch was located off Highway 14 on a gumbo road. If it rained, we knew we were going nowhere unless we walked or rode a horse. It also meant no one would come visiting.

Those were the days we let it all hang loose and didn't worry about how messy the house was. We cut out paper dolls and made houses for them out of Lincoln logs. We made tunnels from blankets and Dad humored us by crawling through them looking for the secret room.

We spent so much of our time with family. Our "happy hour" was after supper when we all lingered over the last crumb of apple pie while Dad and Mother told us stories of the olden days.

Many evenings were spent listening to Dad or Mother read us our favorite stories. We learned dozens of songs and hymns by heart with Mother playing her banjo or harmonica.

The word "bored" was not in my vocabulary. I always found such interesting things to do even if I was alone. I could bake a cake, write a poem, do a puzzle, clip recipes from *Capper's Weekly*, make a scrapbook, go fishing in the dam for bullheads, look at floor plans and pretend I could have anything I wanted in my house, sew a blouse, embroider a dishtowel, or read a good book. In fact, there was never enough time to do all of the fun things I wanted to do.

Sometimes when the weather was gentle the prairie called me. I wandered off to my secret places to be alone. There is something about the prairie sounds that soothe and quiet the spirit. Out on the open prairie the meadowlark sang only for me, the cecropia moth sat on a stalk of wheat beside me, and the tall grasses whispered in my ear. On the Dakota prairies I learned to listen to nature, to God, and to myself.

Years later, my spirit still longs for those quiet times, times away from responsibilities, from noise, from crowds of people. I yearn to sit in the middle of a patch of buffalo grass and pick the wild geraniums and look at the miles and miles of treeless prairies with no houses in sight.

I wonder what people who grew up in a big city long for. I wonder if they, too, don't seek out a quiet corner in a noisy place where they can be alone with themselves and with God.

Country-fied
Autumn

Seize the Moment

As you go for your daily walk, the sights and sounds around you leave no doubt in your mind that autumn is here. Enjoy this moment. Do not think of the winter, the next month with promises of chilly winds. Do not even think of tomorrow.

Feel the sun's warmth on your skin as you take off the flannel jacket you thought you needed on this fall day.

Revel in the autumn's beauty. Embrace the tawny golds, the vivid oranges and scarlets of the leaves before they flutter to the ground. Don't imagine the branches bare and naked against the cold blue sky.

Look at the lush green grass as you mow it one last time. Don't picture it as dry, frozen and brown, but look at it today, growing, alive, a thick and cushy carpet under your feet.

As you dig up the double crimson geranium, don't think about the leaves drying and falling onto the kitchen floor as it goes through the dying and rebirthing process in the shock of transplanting.

Rescue one last red, ripe tomato from the predicted frost, wipe the dirt off on your pants, as most gardeners will do from time to time, and let the juice dribble down your chin as you eat it. No one is looking.

Listen to the cricket sounds. The cricket sings an autumn song, different from the songs of other seasons. Does he know that winter is coming, or does he, too, know how to enjoy this moment without thought of tomorrow?

Tell your friends and your wife or your husband you love them and appreciate them. Right now. Today. Don't wait until the time is right. Don't let tomorrow's maybes rob you of today's joys in a relationship.

Hug your children. Listen to their stories. Laugh at their jokes. Praise your children. Don't wait for them to be better, to do the right thing to make you proud. If you can't praise them for what they've done today, praise them for who they are. Never miss a chance to tell them you love them. Time with them is so short. The huggable, lovable moments are fleeting. Too soon they think they are too big to hug, too independent to need you.

Grasp today's blessing while it is here. Hold on. Do not let it slip away unnoticed while you scurry about to prepare for a winter that may not be.

You do not know the sorrows of tomorrow that await you, nor can you begin to anticipate the joys. All that you have is this moment. Enjoy it. Praise God for it. Grieve in it if you must. Do and feel deeply whatever is appropriate for this time.

Seize the moment.

Cemetery Road

The traffic is heavy on Cemetery Road on a mild October evening. Every 96 seconds we see a car, a pick-up, a roller blader, a bicycle rider, a jogger, a walker, a child pulling a little red wagon, a mother pushing a stroller, a happy unleashed puppy, a speeder, or a patrol car pursuing a speeder.

Serious joggers know the exact distance to walk to fulfill their daily quota of miles. From Highway 281 on North 1st Street to the cemetery - exactly one mile. North to Highway 11 - one-half mile. By completing the trip west on Highway 11 and south on 281 back to the starting point a healthy lap of three miles has been completed. For those less vigorous and dedicated athletes, a brisk walk or a leisurely stroll from any starting and ending point can be rewarding and energizing. The colors of autumn are intense and vivid along the tree-lined road as if God is giving us one more chance at warmth and life before the trees stand naked in the death of winter.

Most of us will be compelled on some of our walks to go into the cemetery, walk between the rows of graves, and read the inscriptions on the headstones. Each headstone marks a birth and death. Some tell a story of a life begun and ended on the same day. Some stories are of tragically short duration, others show incredibly long spans of life. And the laps taken on earth between the beginning and the end of those lives represented by names unknown to us can only be imagined. How many laps were of triumph, victory, and joy, and how many were of sorrow, pain, and disappointment?

We consider our own mortality as we walk between the rows of headstones. If we have loved ones buried there, we shed a tear or two for the precious memories and the sorrow of not having them with us any more.

52

We take comfort in the fact that the seeds that have fallen from the dead flowers in autumn will become next spring's beauty. Those beneath the sod have become everblooming roses in the kingdom of God. We will go through winter as they have gone through death. We will see the rebirth of nature in spring. They, in Christ, have the assurance of eternal life.

The cycle of days are parallel to the seasons of life. Each time of day holds its own beauty, sunrise, noontime, sunset, darkness or moonlight. Spring with new life or beginnings, summer maturity, autumn mellowness, and winter death are all seasons to be celebrated as God's gifts to us.

Joggers make their round trip, returning to their starting point. Those in their final rest have also made their round trip from their Creator, through their laps on earth, and back to rest in their Creator.

We are all traveling on Cemetery Road.

October's Bright Blue Weather

In October, I sometimes think of these lines from a children's poem:
"Come little leaves," said the wind one day.
Let us go out in the meadow and play."

Can we forget ourselves for awhile and completely enjoy this, the most colorful season of the year?

If someone says, "It's a beautiful day," the response is likely to be, "Yah, but we'll pay for this later," as if every blessing requires some recompense, some payment or torture for the pleasure we have now.

Why not rake up a big pile of leaves and roll in them? For people who have small children, that is a legitimate, even a noble thing to do. Why not do it even if we have no small children? Why not keep our sense of playing and have one last fling with the wind and the dancing leaves before we hide in our houses with fluffy comforters up to our ears.

But the farmer has no time to rake the leaves, much less time to play in them. There's digging to do, some combining to finish, and corn to pick.

October's weather is unpredictable, hot one day, cold the next, cold in the early morning, hot by noontime. As the farmer gets ready to go to the cornfield, his wife says, "Wear your parka and take your muscle shirt and your gym shorts. The weather is very changeable in the Dakotas."

They both laugh.

They need to laugh because the corn crop isn't good this year, and if they don't laugh they might cry.

The farmer's wife has no time to play or to enjoy the scenery. She's canning the last of those ugly tomatoes that she picked green when the frost was predicted. They've been sitting in their little flat cardboard boxes on the back porch for two weeks and they definitely aren't red and juicy. She wonders why she's bothering with them, but she hates to throw anything away when there are people in the world who are starving.

Nature's creatures seem to realize that autumn is ending and their days are numbered. The flies are persistent on the screen door, the fat garter snakes are looking for a winter's den. The tame geese are honking and flapping their wings as if they know that winter and the farmer's hatchet are coming and time is running out. In simply observing these living creatures, we can appreciate how great and wonderful God is, how intricate is His plan for creation, for the ebb and flow of the seasons of life.

Through God's gift of October, He gives us one last blessing before Old Man Winter erases the autumn colors in the glorious groves leaving only naked branches. He gives us the bright blue of October to enjoy before the gray ghost envelopes the landscape. We are blessed with one last chance to stroll through the pasture along the creek before snow covers the ground and hides the dormant vegetation.

We can enjoy the blessings of October if only we live in the present and forget to think about the time that is to come.

Understanding Daylight Savings Time

Daylight Savings Time: A plan in which clocks are set one hour ahead of time for a certain period.

Can we really get ahead of time? Does darkness really come an hour later just because our clocks say so? If the clock falls back in October, do our schedules move ahead? Or does time stand still while people move around it? Will the baby wake up earlier or later? If we forget to set our clocks back, will church be almost over when we get there and we will walk in during the benediction or will we have to wait an hour for it to start?

Switching our clocks from Daylight Savings Time to Standard Time and back again is like cutting a piece off one end of the blanket and sewing it onto the other end. We still have the same blanket, it just looks a little funny. There are still 24 hours in a day, the sun doesn't pay any attention to what our clocks say.

One reason for observing Daylight Savings Time was to allow an extra hour of daylight in the evening for recreation. This makes sense for people who work indoors and want to enjoy the outdoors for awhile after work. However, those people who are employed outdoors feel cheated. They get another hour to work before the sun sets.

Maybe we could compromise and set our clocks one-half hour ahead in the spring (or one-half hour behind in the fall) and leave them that way. Then we could be confused all year.

If we save that hour of daylight all summer what will we spend it for in October? It's kind of exciting to set the clock back and withdraw that hour which we deposited in our savings accounts in the spring. Since we can't leave it in savings any longer, we have to decide how to spend it, and spending is easier than saving.

One of my very young nieces was getting ready for school on the Monday morning after the clocks were reset. She said, "Mama, what time is it?"

"It's 7:00 o'clock."

She asked, "But what time is it REALLY?"

Good question!

.....and a Time to Die

The last large leaf fell from the poplar tree and was whisked across the backyard by the brisk autumn wind. The leaf had lived its life of beauty. Its days of providing shade and oxygen to creatures on earth were over and it was ready to return to the soil.

In the span of one month I attended funerals and prayer services for parents of three of my closest friends.

I listened to stories of lives lived in commitment and dedication, stories of people who cared for and loved families, friends, and neighbors. Stories were told of people who showed tremendous strength of character by taking charge in times of adversity or need. There were stories of supportive people who worked quietly in the background without drawing attention to themselves.

I wondered how such quiet, unassuming people could mean so much to so many. They touched lives wherever they were and whatever they did. It is comforting to go to funerals for Christians whose faith was evident not only in words but also in loving and caring deeds.

The heart will be lonely but the head knows that they are in a better place and will not have to endure another long, cold winter of pain and suffering and day-to-day struggles. Even though we will miss them terribly, we can't wish for them to remain here when, like the autumn leaves, their lives of service on earth are over. The tears shed are for ourselves, to acknowlege the emptiness we feel, but our mourning turns into dancing as we rest in the assurance of eternal life in the arms of Jesus.

My mother's funeral five years ago was a celebration of her life. It was a celebration of her love for people, her love for Jesus, and her love of music, laughter, and dancing. She danced her way through life and we could picture her dancing her way into heaven much like Miriam, the sister of Moses, danced to celebrate the Israelites' successful crossing of the Red Sea.

I wonder if, at the end of my life on earth, I will be whisked away like the poplar leaf in my backyard with no trace, no memory, no mark that I had made a difference. Will there be a celebration of my life at my funeral? Will anyone have good memories or funny stories to share? Have I done anything worth remembering?

By the grace of God, there will be a celebration!

The Winter List

When the leaves have fallen, the wind chills to the bone, and the geese are flying south, you know it's time to make that list and get a stash of supplies, just in case........

If you don't stock up, you might find yourself alone in a three-day blizzard with nothing to do and no food in the house, three kids, two dogs and a cat, all screaming, barking, or meowing for something to eat, or something to do, or begging to go outside when you know that it's not possible or wise for them to do so, but you certainly wish they could because if they don't go away for awhile, you will not be responsible for your actions or for the nasty things you are going to say if they keep bugging you.

So you get out a long piece of paper and list the things you need to get so you will be properly prepared this winter.

You need a couple bushels of munchies to hide in places where no one can find them, like in the clothes hamper or in their clean socks drawers. Powdered milk, extra bags of flour and sugar, an outdoor extension cord, another string of tree lights to put up in case there's another nice day, and the list grows long.

Better get some jigsaw puzzles. Nobody will ever, ever do one of those unless there's a blizzard, then they have to have the kitchen table full of 1,000 puzzle pieces so you have no place to roll out those homemade noodles that you never, never make except when there's a blizzard.

You saw an ad the other day for one of those kerosene space heaters. That goes on your list along with kerosene. You wonder where in the world you'll buy kerosene, but put it on the list anyway. If they sell heaters, they must know where you can buy kerosene.

Yes, and batteries for every flashlight in the house and one for the big flashlight in the car. You probably want to check the supply of candles. Even if the electricity doesn't go off, they're kind of nice for atmosphere.

And thinking of the electricity going off reminds you of the terrible time you had last year when you put a pan of hotdogs on the stove to cook but forgot the electricity was off, so you put them on a paper plate and stuck them in the microwave and said, "Well, duh! I guess if the stove doesn't work neither will the microwave," so you ate them cold. You think about looking for the camp stove in the garage then remember what the garage looks like and add camp stove to your list.

You wonder where the scoop shovel is then remember that your husband put it in his pickup when he left for work. You will have to get another one and maybe a couple of smaller shovels for the kids to use when they "help" you shovel the sidewalk.

You think, "I have my list complete. Maybe I'd better make a trip in to town right now while I'm thinking about it."

You bundle up the kids and yourself, find your purse and the checkbook and head for the door.

As you open the door, a gust of icy wind blows in. The snow is coming down sideways and you can't see the neighbor's house across the road. The dogs start to bark, the cat wants out, the kids start begging for a snack.....

Soup Time

The first snowflakes fall in late autumn. They whiten the still-green grass beside the parking lot adjacent to my workplace. The fresh, crisp air nips my nose and makes my fingers tingle as I scrape the unwelcome frost from my windshield. I turn the heater to vent to keep the windows clear and I shiver from the cold blast.

The eastern sky looks cold and unfriendly with the slate blues and mauves of the reluctant sunrise.

Autumn is always too short and as usual, the first snowfall catches me by surprise. I am unprepared and unwilling to deal with the cold, the snow, the sleet, and the ice as I drive to and from work at my third-shift job.

I turn my thoughts toward home. I stop to fill the gas tank and buy a few groceries so I won't have to leave my house once I am settled in. I can't wait to get home to the warmth and comfort of my kitchen. Even though I don't usually enjoy cooking, I feel an urgency to get out the big stainless steel soup pot and set stewing beef to simmering on the back burner while I read the morning paper and sip hot flavored coffee.

It's Saturday, my only day off, and I savor every moment.

There is comfort in the fact that no lawn cries to be mowed, no flower gardens beg for weeding, and no produce is ready to be picked and canned.

I curl up on the couch under the big granny-square afghan my daughter crocheted and leaf through my pile of quilting magazines to study the latest trends in color and design. I choose the next two quilts I'm going to start when we have that three-day blizzard in January. I call a friend, do a crossword puzzle, dream about the days when I can spend more time at home.

Tomorrow night I'll join the real world again-the world of quotas, time sheets, and factory noises that mingle with the always- too-loud, ever-present contemporary music blaring through overhead speakers.

But today, without a hint of guilt, I will lounge in quiet solitude with my coffee, my magazines, and the promise of tasty winter stew made from summer vegetables.

No Gender Neutrality in Hunting and Fishing

Once upon a time on the opening Saturday of deer hunting season, a man took his wife with him. She wanted to spend quality time with her husband, to enjoy with him the crisp fall air, to sit with him in his secluded shelter belt while he waited for The Buck, the biggest he had ever seen. Even though common sense told him this was not a good idea, he relented.

He parked the truck at the end of the shelter belt and they made their way soundlessly through the trees until they came to the spot where he knew The Buck would appear. They sat motionless, blending in with the fall foliage, for hours. Then, there he was. The Buck. Right in line for the perfect shot. The hunter slowly, carefully, raised his rifle, and aimed. Perfect!

Just as he was ready to squeeze the trigger, his wife jumped up, flapped her arms wildly, and screamed, "Run, Bambi, run!"

The hunter exploded with several paragraphs of colorful expletives which, loosely interpreted, meant, "Love of My Life, why did you do that?"

With tears rolling down her cheeks she said, "How could you shoot anything that beautiful?"

On his way to the shelter belt the next Saturday he gave her $100 and dropped her off at the Quilter's Kozy Korner where they were offering all-day classes on stack and whack quilting techniques. He figured it would be the best mileage he ever got for $100.

Even though a guy complains that he can't find any girl who likes hunting and fishing, does he really want a girl who picks up nightcrawlers and baits her own hook? Wouldn't he rather be a big hero and do it for her while she watches admiringly and says, "Eyew!"?

In my opinion, fishing should be done on a hot summer day when I can walk barefoot along the river bank or dig my toes into the cool sand at the edge of a lake. Perhaps while waiting for a fish to bite I can do a little handwork on that doily I started a year ago. If I don't watch too closely maybe I won't have to take a hook out of a bluegill's upper lip.

For guys, however, the thrill is in ice-fishing. They start checking the depth of the ice about two days after the first frost. They work for two months of week-ends pounding nails into some used 2 x 4's and chunks of plywood left over from last year's garage building project to make something which resembles an over-sized outhouse. When the big day arrives, the ice is finally thick enough, they haul the shack out on the lake or river, hang a Terry Redlin print on the wall, light the propane heater, try out the new ice auger, and sit on homemade stools to wait for a fish to find that tiny hole in the ice.

Now tell me, what self-respecting woman would want to hunker down on a remnant of lime green shag carpet, huddle under a scuzzy buffalo robe, and play poker on an overturned bait bucket?

I know people are going to tell me that they personally know of, or at least have heard of, at least one woman who genuinely loves hunting and fishing. I won't argue the point, but I'll bet if she truly loves the hunting and fishing life, she will fall in love with a man who loves to quilt.

Spending a Bazaar Week-end

Let me check out the area papers to see what's happening this mid-November week-end. What activities or events would be appropriate for a conservative Republican with a German Lutheran heritage?

There's hot oil wrestling. That looks disgusting. How about a movie starring John Travolta? I rather like John but I notice it's rated R. I haven't recovered from the R-movie I saw three years ago.

Hmmmm, this looks interesting. The Ultimate 5 Male Dancers. I don't think so.

Now here are some things I might like–a church bazaar, a floral shop open house, and a Creative Hands Craft Show. This will be enjoyable and maybe I'll get some good ideas for my own craft business.

Off I go to the church bazaar. I see the usual assortment of Norwegian goodies, potted plants, quilts made by the quilting ladies, and even a pair of miniature tatted slippers. I haven't seen tatting for years. The amount of talent exhibited here is amazing.

The floral shop array of ornately decorated trees is riveting. I can hardly focus on individual items because of the impact of the over-all effect. I gaze in wonder at the artistic ability shown in the displays.

The Creative Hands Craft Show is so crowded that I feel like a salmon swimming upstream. Where do people come up with all these ideas? There are weed pictures, plaques for every conceivable occasion or non-occasion, and rag Santas perched amidst the ceramic Thanksgiving turkeys. There's a horse for a carousel, and jewelry made of rocks and feathers with decorated wooden boxes for storing it. A flower-pot Rudolph the Red-nosed Reindeer winks at me beside a wooden-shoe vase filled with fabric flowers.

Angels are big this year. I've seen lace angels, marshmallow angels, mop angels, rafia angels, wheat angels, and clothespin angels.

The permeating scent of eucalyptus is giving me a headache and making my eyes water.

I see so many gorgeous items which I'd love to have but with so many choices in front of me I can't make a decision. I buy one huge bag of homemade noodles and fight my way to the door, feeling claustrophobic.

There are still 49 shopping days until Christmas and I'm already suffering from a severe case of Christmas craft overkill.

Is it too late to buy a ticket to see the Ultimate 5?

For What Do We Give Thanks?

Do we have a spirit of thanksgiving as the holiday season approaches? Or are we so used to harboring negative thoughts and complaining about our situations that we find it difficult to be thankful for everyday blessings and God's provision not only for our needs, but also for many of our wants?

We become upset about the piles of wet towels and dirty laundry but forget to give thanks for the supplies of soap and water which enable us to be clean. In some countries, people walk as far as six miles a day in search of drinking water. We complain about the price of fuel oil while people are freezing to death in the streets.

We put off washing the sinkful of dirty dishes and forget to be thankful that we have eaten, and that we have enough dishes to set another table. We consider leftovers an inferior meal while in most countries of the world there are no leftovers.

We want to re-decorate our homes when we become tired of the furniture, or the carpet and drapes are a little faded. Yet many people consider themselves fortunate if they have a quilt to spread on the ground at night.

We replace our two-year-old winter coat because it's out of style. Someone in the world would be glad to have the one we discard.

Our children complain about school, but in many countries of the world, education is a luxury which few can afford.

Every year we eat our traditional dinner of turkey, dressing, sweet-potatoes, mashed potatoes, three salads, relish tray, cranberries, and a choice of three kinds of pie, and try not to think about the children whose pain comes from empty stomachs and not from stomachs that are too full.

How can we be thankful for bountiful blessings while others lack even the barest essentials? How can we look at pictures of starving people with haunting eyes and say, "Thank you, God, that I'm not one of them," without doing something about their pain and poverty?

In a sermon on this topic, one of my pastors said that the media depicts such horrendous needs in the world that we become immobilized and think that anything we can do is insignificant and won't make a difference.

He said, "You can't solve all of the world's problems, but you *can* take care of what God puts in front of you today."

Sadie's Radical Christmas

It was November first. Sadie was running errands and window shopping. She felt depressed again. The holiday season was approaching. The children had already worn out the Christmas catalogs with their looking and had worn out Sadie with their wishing and begging.

As she looked at one flashing window display after another, she muttered mentally, "I can't believe it. The merchants have barely washed the Halloween soap off their windows before the Christmas trees go up and my ears are assaulted with the strains of 'Have a Holly, Jolly Christmas' blaring from the loud speakers. I haven't even bought my Thanksgiving turkey yet. Thanksgiving! Whatever happened to Thanksgiving? When I was a child we took things as they came. Didn't even think about Christmas until after Thanksgiving. Apparently we want Christmas in November."

She trudged up one street and down another. She had an idea! The more she walked, the more she thought, and soon a slight smile turned the downward corners of her mouth upward.

In a while she bustled from shop to shop in the mall. The stores were not crowded. It was a good thing, because every once in awhile Sadie laughed out loud or hummed a little tune as she did her errands and finished her shopping. Her depression miraculously lifted.

Thanksgiving Eve the children were sent to bed at 8:00 o'clock. They fussed and carried on, but Homer said, "Kids, mind your mother!"

He was an old-fashioned father and what mother said was law. But when Sadie sent Homer upstairs to his office at 8:30, he fussed. For just a little while. After all, he had lived with Sadie long enough to expect the unexpected from her and he was often amazed and amused at the unusual things she did.

When everyone was out of the way, Sadie brought the Christmas tree out of the garage, set it up, and decorated it. She took all the boxes full of presents out of their secret hiding places where they had been stored since November first. She wrapped and taped and tied and put them under the tree. She made candy and goodies. By the time she crawled into bed, it was 3:30 a.m.

Thanksgiving morning Sadie leaped out of bed at 6:00 a.m., put on her housecoat, and went flying through the house yelling, "Wake up! Wake up! We're celebrating Jesus's birthday. Wake up!"

The children were stunned, but elated. They gathered around the lighted tree in their pajamas, looking like little cherubs. They were amazingly well-behaved. They hadn't had time to get excited or hyper. They opened their presents, from youngest to oldest in turn. Sadie opened hers, too. Since she had bought her own gifts, she got exactly what she had on her Christmas list.

Sadie made each one of the children promise very solemnly that they would not tell a soul they had already had their Christmas. They had a lot of fun pretending to their friends that they were still wishing for things that they already had.

When Sadie visited with her friends as the number of shopping days before Christmas dwindled, and her friends were frazzled and frayed over Christmas crowds and their hyperactive, over-stimulated children, she said, "It really is a hectic time, isn't it?" but inside, she was calm, serene, and smiling.

She felt especially good because there had been no unnecessary last-minute impulse buying, so she had $100 of Christmas money left over. She wrote a check for World Hunger and placed it in the church offering plate.

On Christmas morning, Sadie got up early, put the turkey in the oven, made pumpkin pies, and cooked cranberries, dressing, and mashed potatoes. She set the table with Thanksgiving napkins, the cornucopia centerpiece, and the turkey salt and pepper shakers. As they bowed their heads for grace, Homer prayed, "Thank you, Lord, for providing for us so abundantly. Thank you for sending your Son for our salvation. And thank you for my wonderful, unpredictable wife."

He winked at Sadie.

The children smiled and felt all warm and cozy inside.

Country-fied Winter

Blizzard Blues

Howling winds of a blizzard always catch me by surprise even though I know that winter happens any time after September first in the Midwest.

When the northwest wind drives the icy snow pellets against my house, I go into fits of restlessness. I pace the floor between bedroom, living room, and kitchen, peering out of the frosted windows as though looking out and pacing are going to change the weather or make me feel better.

I open the refrigerator door. There's nothing in there except orange juice, milk, catsup, and fourth-day leftover stir-fry. How about the cupboard? One can of pork and beans, a nearly-empty bag of rice, and half a package of stale crackers. I did it again. I forgot to buy my be-prepared-for-a-blizzard supply of groceries.

I can at least make myself a pot of coffee, if the electricity doesn't go off. Oh, Lord, what will I do if the electricity goes off? I wonder where I put the flashlight. I think I left it in the car. Better bring it in. I think I have some candles in the closet. Better find them. Hope I remembered to get matches.

I wonder if it's let up any. What if this turns into a three-day blizzard?

This pacing is ridiculous. Let me try to find something fun and interesting to do. Wish I had a good book that I haven't read. I forgot to stop at the library. I can sew as long as I have electricity. Guess I'll get that quilt put together. Oh, I forgot. I'm a yard short of the mauve fabric I need. Can't work on that project.

Maybe I should clean out my closets. That would take my mind off the storm. Cleaning out closets is even more depressing than the storm, but here goes. I'll throw out or give away the stuff I don't wear. That cuts my wardrobe by half. Now I'll take out the clothes I don't like. That eliminates half of the half and leaves me with two skirts, two sweaters, two pairs of pants, two blouses, and one dress. I'll have to wash clothes every five days, but I'll always be wearing something I like.

It's still snowing out and the wind is stronger. I can't see the house across the street.

I know. I'll get out my pictures and photo albums. I've been trying for years to get them sorted. For some twisted reason, I have an emotional attachment to every picture in my collection and can't bear to throw any of them away.

Here's one of my niece with her oatmeal bowl on her head. She'd be pleased to know I still have that. This one with the back half of the dog and a couch with dirty socks draped over the arm is a real treasure. Likewise this one of my son crossing his eyes and making bunny ears over his cousin's head. Here are three pictures of Grandma with her hair in pink curlers, wearing her ragged chenille housecoat, rolled down stockings, and fluffy slippers. One of those is too many. Here's the seventh picture of me trying to get out of the picture. Lovely. Who took this one of me in my mini-skirt? I definitely should have gotten out of that picture. Who's this leaning over my car engine? I don't recognize the hind end.

I really should throw all of these away, but if I do, I won't have anything to do during the next blizzard.

Oops. There goes the electricity. It's too dark to see anything. Have to take a nap whether I want one or not.

Too bad.

The Christmas Form Letter

Stella's Christmas card was always in the mail the day after Thanksgiving. Every year it was gilded with gold, the biggest card in the mailbox.

The picture included with the card showed an elegantly decorated home with Stella and Don happily smiling. Billy, dressed in his Sunday suit, charmingly imitated his father's pose. When the twins, Jean and Jan, were little, they were picture-perfect in their patent leather shoes and red velvet dresses with matching bows in their curly blond hair.

The letter was typed in fancy script on red or green paper and decorated with elaborate computer graphics. It brought everyone up-to-date on all of the many activities of the family.

Don was a loan officer at the bank and was being rapidly promoted with the accompanying salary increases. He was president of the Chamber of Commerce, active on his church council, involved with the parent's organization at the junior high school and spent his week-ends helping Stella around the house.

Stella's home-based business in graphic design was flourishing. She had several major accounts and had just signed a contract with a well-known magazine. She, too, was active in the community. She volunteered at a local nursing home once a week, sang in the church choir, and spent a lot of time chauffeuring the children to their activities.

Billy was a straight-A student, a member of the basketball team that went to the state tournament, liked hunting and fishing, had a paper route and a part-time job so he could buy his car, and was already trying to decide which college he might want to attend.

Stella and Don tried to encourage the twins to choose different activities so they didn't depend on each other too much. Jean had first chair in the clarinet section in the junior high band. Jan was a soloist in the high school swing choir even though she was still in junior high. They were both honor students, but Jean excelled in math and science, and Jan was interested in creative writing and design. Jean was on the volleyball team, Jan took ballet and piano lessons.

Every summer the family took a two-week vacation. At various times they had toured the Rocky Mountains, Washington, D.C., Nashville, and Disneyland. Several vacations were spent camping in northern Minnesota and the Black Hills.

Last week there was a plain, small card in the mailbox. There was no picture, no long letter, just two short sentences at the bottom of the card.

"I am divorced. Please pray for me." Stella.

The Miracle of Christmas

Al was alone that Christmas. For the first time in his life he felt old and lonely. As he traipsed through the mall, stopping in shop after shop, he tried to think what the grandchildren might like for Christmas. He had no idea. Elsa had always done the shopping. She loved Christmas and doing for others. They had money then, money that they had earned together, working side by side on the farm. There was no "yours" or "mine." The money, the outside work, and the housework were all "ours" and they shared everything. Elsa, his wife of 44 years died in October after a long and painful illness. The money was gone. The insurance didn't cover the horrendous expenses of hospitalizations and treatments. The savings accounts and investments were depleted, even the retirement nest egg had to be used.

As Al wandered from one display to another amid the noise, the mobs, children begging and whining, he was overcome with a sense of hopelessness. He was astonished at the price of everything. How had Elsa managed to shop so wisely and make the money stretch as she had?

He thought, "There is nothing my children or grandchildren need or want that my few dollars can buy."

The brashness of the red and green displays was outdone only by the volume of the "Twelve Days of Christmas" blaring from loudspeakers everywhere. There were decorations from floors to ceilings. Merchandise was spilling out into the aisles and hallways of the mall. The lights were flashing and blinking until everything became a blur.

Al felt dizzy and disoriented. His head ached and he thought to himself, "I can't stand one more minute of bell ringing and crowds."

Then he wandered by chance into a quiet little craft shop and was drawn to a simple homemade creche with hand carved figures and weathered wood. His eyes rested on the simple figure of the baby in the manger and he saw a single beam of light shining toward heaven. A quiet tear rolled down Al's cheek as he thought, "God knew that I needed a special sign tonight to remind me that God gave us himself in the form of a human child. I have nothing to give my family except myself. Now I know what I will give them for Christmas."

He went into the nearest variety store and bought a dozen blank tapes. He walked, almost ran, out of the mall and started to think about the things that were important in his life, the things he had to offer that no money could buy. He knew his children would appreciate his talents, and that someday his grandchildren also would appreciate them. When he got home, he took the fiddle out of the case, put the tape player on "record," and taped three of his favorite songs. He sang the song that his brother had sung for him and Elsa at their wedding. He sang on perfect pitch in his deep clear voice. He recited poetry he had memorized in a little country school years ago. Humor was such a part of their daily lives so Al included funny stories about Elsa trying to ride a horse and about the times the kids did naughty things. The grandchildren might like to hear that their parents weren't so perfect after all. Al chuckled to himself at some of these memories. He ended his program with a reading of the Christmas story in his powerful, expressive voice.

With a song in his heart, Al wrapped the 12 identical tapes, one for each of his children and grandchildren. On each card he wrote in his perfect penmanship, "This year I have nothing to offer you but myself and my love."

His children thought his gift was the best of all.

What Have We Done To Christmas?

"I hate Christmas."

Have you ever said that? Or thought it?

Christmas is supposed to be the happiest, most joyful time of the year. But many people never experience the perfect Christmas, the perfect dinner, the perfect gift. For many, the holiday season brings sad memories. The loss of a family member creates a big empty hole in the middle of the family gathering and dampens the spirit of celebration. For families of divorce, there is confusion about who celebrates what with whom. It is not a perfect time. It is not a storybook celebration.

What about the pre-adolescent boy who doesn't want to go back to school after Christmas vacation because he knows that at least one teacher will ask the kids to tell what they got for Christmas? He already knows that his friends got computer software and ice-skates. He got pajamas and a bag of one-size-fits all socks.

And can we handle one more, "Oh-I-really-shouldn't-but-it's-all-so-good-I'll-start-my-diet-after-New-Year's-Day" as Auntie reaches for the English toffee to top off the fondant nut roll and Martha Washington bon-bons.

People start looking for ideas in September. There are those few rare souls who have all of their Christmas done by September 1st. How can we be done with Christmas by September 1st?

During October, people are looking for Christmas cards and things to make so they can avoid the pressure of the last minute rush.

In November, they're taking out Christmas loans which they can't afford, to pay for gifts that cost too much, to give to people who already have everything they need. But they HAVE to give SOMETHING.

By December 15th, people are becoming frantic and upset because they still have so much to do and not enough time in which to do it all. They feel guilty for not being able to give their children everything they want. At the same time, they are feeling guilty because the budget is shot until the end of March.

By December 24th, customers are grabbing an unnecessary box of candy because at the eleventh hour, Great Uncle Jim pulled in and they don't have a gift for him.

The clerks have been crabby for three weeks. After all, they went to gift shows in June, placed orders in July, marked merchandise in August, and did last minute inventories and orders for more in September. For the last three months, they have unpacked, displayed, sold, and wrapped. They are ready to bite the next person who asks if the chocolate Santas are half-price yet. At 4 p.m. they go home to try to prepare a joyful time for their own families, and they can't even enjoy the day because they know that on the 26th they will face the yearly nightmare - a mob of unhappy receivers. The clerks will have to look at those same gifts again as they refund and exchange - with a smile, of course.

So where is the JOY in all of this? When did we decide to bury Jesus in red ribbon, wrapping paper, tinsel, neon lights, chocolate chips, and sweetened condensed milk? When did we lose sight of the true Gift of Christmas?

Do we dare in our own lives to say, "Enough! I quit. Just give me silence and peace and worship this Christmas?"

Do we dare to call a moratorium on Christmas decorations, lights, and holiday displays until after Thanksgiving, the one wonderful holiday that has remained virtually non-commercial?

Do we dare to give purely out of love and refuse to give out of a sense of duty or even desperation? Do we dare to give anonymously to someone who may not have the joy of Christmas otherwise? Could we ask each member of the family to forego one gift and use that money to work together to make a layette for a baby born to a mother who has nothing with which to clothe her child?

Do we dare to make one less salad for Christmas dinner and give that $5 to our church's world hunger appeal? Do we dare to simplify our Christmas so that we have time to gather around the piano to sing carols, to worship at candlelight service, to take time to walk in the moonlight, look at the stars and simply capture the wonder of the moment? Do we dare to focus on the one Perfect Gift, the Gift God sent all of us, the gift of His perfect Son Jesus?

Do we dare?

Christmas Nostalgia

In this essay, there is no moral, no surprise ending, just snippets of childhood experiences which might trigger a memory or two of your own.

Christmases of years ago seemed simpler, less materialistic, than they do now. Perhaps things always seem simpler in retrospect; perhaps things really are more complicated now.

In the living room of our little three-room house, we hung thick red streamers from corner to corner and looped them up in the center with a bell of red tissue paper which folded out, honeycomb fashion. We cut and pasted long paper chains from construction paper to hang in the doorway with another bell in the center.

We had no fireplace but my two sisters and I hung our long tan stockings on the back of a chair and were delighted with the bulges of oranges, candy, and presents we found in the morning. I don't remember what kind of stocking my younger brother hung up. Maybe by the time he was old enough to celebrate Christmas we had a tree and didn't hang the stockings any more.

The tree was little. There wasn't enough room in our small house for a big tree. If its branches were thin, we filled in the gaps with silver tinsel, lots of silver tinsel. We made garlands of popcorn and cranberries to hang on the tree. The most wonderful decoration we had on the tree after we got electricity was the string of candle bubble lights.

On Christmas Eve, Dad joked, "I guess we'd better set a bear trap tonight. There's going to be a bearded old man in a red suit prowling around in our yard."

This brought choruses of, "No, Daddy! No, Daddy!"

We usually opened our gifts on Christmas morning, but one year we were going to leave early on Christmas Day to visit relatives so we wanted to open them Christmas Eve. Dad decided we should all ride with him to the mailbox to mail some letters and wouldn't you know? Santa came while we were gone.

The boxes of presents from uncles and aunts were hidden in the closet in the old wash house. We sneaked in there to shake the boxes and try to feel what was inside, but the boxes were securely taped and tied. We wondered how Santa knew they were in the closet.

I remember eating black walnut candy from Uncle Curt and Aunt Mary in California. I've never seen that type of candy in any store in the Midwest. I remember getting baking utensils from Uncle Honey and Aunt Ermina because they knew we liked to bake and decorate goodies. I remember magazine subscriptions from Uncle Bill and Aunt Bay in Rapid City.

Mama insisted that we write thank you notes for our gifts. I asked her what I should write to Aunt Nelle and she said, "You can write, 'Thank you for the lovely stationery'."

I stubbornly said, "I'm not going to use that stupid word 'lovely'."

When I mentioned my naughtiness to her years later, she said, "I don't remember that."

Isn't it strange what small details we remember sometimes, when the more important events are forgotten? Yet what more important lesson could Mama have taught us than to be thankful and appreciate what others did for us?

The highlight of our Christmases were the programs at Pleasant Vale, our little country school. I remember my brother dressed up like Frosty the Snowman. We performed in plays, spoke our pieces, and sang all of the verses to the old familiar carols. I remember the really special year when Casey Tibbs, World Champion Cowboy, sat in the audience dressed in his best suit to watch his nephew in the program. Life didn't get any better than that!

I began to suspect the Santa hoax when he signed his name with a capital C with a curvy tail on it the way Mama made her capital C's. I followed Dad around while he was doing his chores and asked, "There is no Santa Claus, is there?"

He just said, "What do *you* think?"

I said, "I think he's pretend but pretending is fun."

Mama taught us her favorite Christmas carols while strumming the banjo. She sang "Stille Nacht" to us in German as her mother had sung it to her. She read us the Christmas story and made sure that we understood that God sent His Son to be our Saviour. Her favorite scripture was John 3:16, the verse of salvation by grace.

I remember the way Dad laughed whenever he or one of his neighbors said, "I wish you a *prosperous* New year."

Farmers in those days were anything *but* prosperous yet they were always able to laugh about their circumstances.

I hope those of you who have been faithful readers of "Country-fied" also have wonderful memories of Christmas Past and that you will continue to pass memorable traditions on to the next generations.

I wish you a Merry Christmas and a *prosperous* New Year.

Winter Doldrums

Christmas is over.

The glitz and glitter are done for another year.

We find some comfort in the fact that we won't have to listen to one more bad rendition of "White Christmas" or "Grandma Got Runover by a Reindeer."

The dog is eating the last of the turkey and dressing. The gifts have been returned, exchanged, put in drawers, or hung in closets. The pine needles are clinging stubbornly to the carpet.

The house is unbearably quiet and empty with the company gone. Grandma has polished off the last of the eggnog and is sleeping in her recliner.

The Christmas boxes of decorations have been hauled to the attic.

Everyone can feel a long winter chest cold settling in and the kids have the flu.

The outdoor lights aren't turned on any more. The December electricity bill was out-of-sight and lest we become too positive and cheerful, the mailman blessed us with the Visa bill, the IRS forms, and the pink slips from the Treasurer's office telling us the real estate taxes are due.

The days are short and nights are cold. January, February and March have to be endured before we have something to look forward to, like Easter in April or the first robin in the spring.

But life goes on. We couldn't bear to have the intensity of the holidays all year. The winter months can be a time of quiet contemplation and renewal of our weary spirits, a time of freedom from busyness, a time to do unexpected kindnesses and finish projects begun in the midst of wild activity.

Let's not pack God away with the nativity scene, but keep the warmth of Him inside, a light to keep our spirits burning brightly when the world seems only gray and hopeless. We may have to look a little harder to see evidence that He is with us, but He hasn't gone away.

The seed catalog came in the mail today, the vivid burnt orange, crimson, and purple sunset graced the western horizon from north to south this evening, the white-sale circular advertised that the bedroom set we wanted and didn't get is now on sale for 50 percent off, and a child set the table and took out the garbage without being asked.

There is hope.

Resolution Reruns

Recently I was having lunch with my friend. She said very seriously, "My New Year's resolution is to finish every project I've started and use every piece of fabric in my house before I buy anything more to make."

We laughed till the tears ran down our cheeks because both of us have made that same resolution for the past five years. It's impossible for people who are into crafts or sewing to complete even one project without dreaming up three more.

I got motivated during my fall housecleaning to clean out the project closets. As I pulled boxes and bags from shelves I piled the projects according to priority in my sewing room. I put the least important against the walls, the most pressing in the middle of the floor. I reasoned that if I tripped over them every time I went in there to iron, I would be likely to do them soon. That assumption, of course, was based on the premise that I would iron.

I found such interesting projects while I was cleaning. I found yardages of double-knit, one piece with a flare-leg pants pattern still attached. There were quilt blocks my mother-in-law and I had cut out and embroidered. She's been dead for 16 years. I found three bags of quilt pieces without enough mauve to finish the quilt top. I'll have to buy a couple more yards. Then I'll have mauve pieces left over so I'll have to buy something to go with the mauve to make another project. I walked down memory lane when I ran across the box of my son's T-shirts which I was saving for a "Grandma's Memory" quilt. I planned to cut out the emblems and logos and applique them to a sheet so the grandsons can sleep under memories when they visit Grandma. Since I have no grandsons yet, there's no hurry with that project. Besides, I used the sheet I bought for it when I made my Amish quilt.

I found the yoke of gingham checked fabric that I smocked for my daughter when she was three years old. She strictly forbids me to tell her age any more, but she's been self-supporting for over a dozen years.

There was the printed jacket which I started and got as far as the shoulder pads and couldn't figure out how to put them in without getting wrinkles and puckers. I'll çonquer that project this year. I found one cotton gabardine suit cut out, pattern pieces still pinned on, and one piece of wool fabric and lining for another suit. I need the wool suit now, but I can't cut into the wool until I sew the cotton pants to see if the pattern fits. I'd rather ruin the cotton than the wool, so the wool will have to wait.

And so on a cold, stormy, winter day-off, you might find me sitting in the middle of my sewing room floor, looking through my four cardboard boxes, three suitcases, and eight grocery bags full of lengths of assorted fabrics, with no particular pattern or project in mind. But it's fun to look and dream. As one of my seamstressing friends says, "Looking at fabrics and patterns is almost as good as having them done."

She also has a bumper sticker that says, "The one who dies with the most fabric wins."

I'm definitely a contender in that race.

What do you want to bet that my next year's New Year's resolution will be, "Put all of these projects back in the closet where they belong?

Out with the Old, In with the New

It was New Year's Eve. Dad and Mama considered the choices for celebrating. They could stay home, be warm and toasty by the fireplace while they watched Guy Lombardo and all the people with their little party hats and kazoos in Times Square, or they could go to the church's annual New Year's Eve party. The twins, Hayley and Clem, were young enough to get excited about the church party. They were young enough to get excited about going ANY place. Mama and Dad liked the fellowship and the informal, homey atmosphere of church so that was their choice.

To Dan and Cora, the church party sounded totally boring. Dan decided to go cruising, since he had recently become the proud owner of a driver's license. Cora went along with him even though his driving scared the wits out of her. At least it would be more fun than a boring church party. They picked up a couple of friends and cruised Main Street and a few other well-known roads looking for the party or for someone who knew where the party was.

At the stop light they met Eddy with a carload of his friends. They were looking for the party, too, but no one seemed to know where it was. After about an hour of cruising they were all bored. So everyone in Dan's car and everyone in Eddy's car decided to descend on the church party. They acted nonchalant as if they had planned all along to be there.

Hayley immediately signed up for the potato relay, Clem opted for a serious game of pinochle with the grown-ups. Dads challenged their sons to a wild game of Pit in which the Dads got carried away and yelled so loudly they embarrassed their wives. This was one of those rare times when the men forgot to discuss politics, crops, or scandals, and reverted to being children again.

The high-schoolers got out their favorite board games and didn't even protest when younger children and older women wanted to join them in Pictionary, Yahtze, Outburst, and Trivial Pursuit. They avoided playing Bible Trivial Pursuit with Grandma, because she always won. How *did* she remember all those minute details?

There were many time-outs for pop breaks and loading and reloading the plates with fudge, chocolate chip cookies, peanut brittle, caramel corn, nachos and cheese dip, lefse, pfefferneusse, salted-in-the-shell peanuts, and pretzels dipped in almond bark, as if they hadn't had enough holiday goodies already.

At midnight, they ushered Father Time out the door and welcomed the New Year Baby with as much noise and commotion as the revelers in Times Square.

At 12:10 a.m., they became silent as they filed reverently into the sanctuary. They sat in a circle, joined hands and sang "Auld Lang Syne," then prayed silently as the pastor gave them communion by candlelight. Mama forgot about all of the tragedies and heartaches of the past year as she looked at her children's faces silhouetted in the half-light. She saw in each of them the assurance and the promise of blessings to come and her heart was filled with peace in the joy of the present.

Who Is Your Valentine?

When we think of valentines do we conjure up warm, fuzzy feelings involving someone resembling our favorite TV personality who is a perfect 10?

When we think of the word love do we think of it as something that just happens, and if it happens, does it make us feel good, and if it feels good, it must be right?

Do we think of love as action and self-sacrifice? How about putting the needs and wants of others ahead of our own? These are not popular concepts in an era in which so much emphasis has been put on self-image, self-realization, self-improvement, and self-analysis.

In the real world, most of the people we deal with on a daily basis are not perfect 10's, in fact they are probably not even close.

St. Valentine was a Christian martyr of the third century. The word martyr does not give us warm, fuzzy thoughts.

If we look around us, we can see many examples of real love. These people have not given their lives in the way that St. Valentine did, but they have done the responsible thing and perhaps that is really the essence of love.

We see the commitment of a wife who goes to the nursing home every day to feed her husband and hold his hand, even though he may have become mean-spirited or difficult and is not the same person as he was when he was young.

A mother wears the same dress and the old shoes every Sunday so her son can have braces on his teeth.

A father works overtime to buy his daughter the prom dress of her dreams.

A man spends time helping his injured neighbor plant his crops and expects no payment for his labor.

A child puts part of his allowance in the World Hunger box in Sunday School.

Foster parents give a loving home to children in need.

A gifted and caring teacher spends many hours after school, on weekends, and during the summer to upgrade skills and find ideas and activities to help children learn.

Volunteers work to beautify their communities or promote businesses.

Grandparents spend hours of their time taking care of grandchildren, giving them a sense of stability and security which they might not have otherwise.

A special friend listens and means it when she says she will keep a conversation in confidence.

Someone sends an anonymous gift to someone in need and finds great joy in never being found out.

A person who is homebound finds ways to encourage and befriend others with written messages and intercessory prayer.

There are those in the community who help serve Christmas dinners, donate to the food pantry, volunteer for the ambulance crew, donate blood, recycle, and the list goes on and on.

Maybe this Valentine's Day we should each ask ourselves, "Who are the real Valentines in my life?" and "Who needs me to be their Valentine?"

Social Life in a Small Town

In a small town, no matter how short our list, we normally allow at least an hour for grocery shopping because we always find a friend or neighbor who wants to talk.

This winter when the farmer and his wife finally get plowed out, they head for town to replenish their supplies and get home again before the next blizzard blows in. They allow a little more time than usual on this February day because they will run into people they haven't seen since Christmas and they are hungry for conversation.

They have forgotten how to talk about anything except the weather.

In the fresh produce aisle, the women talk to anyone who will listen.

"I usually cook a big kettle of soup during a blizzard. We've had so many blizzards, I'm running out of soup recipes."

"Won't need to worry about planting our gardens until the Fourth of July this year. It will take that long for all of the snow to thaw. I'm going to run over to the hardware store and get some of those ten-for-a-dollar packets of garden seeds and some potting soil. Maybe I'll feel better if I get my hands in some dirt and watch for something green."

"I know what you mean. I hate golf, but I watch golf tournaments so I can remember what grass looks like."

In the beverage aisle the wife says, "We ran out of coffee. Both my husband and I went through caffeine withdrawal. It was not pretty."

Women discuss purchases in the paper products section.

"Gotta stock up on toilet paper. Can't use the old Sears catalog like Grandpa and Grandma did in the outhouse."

"What do you do to pass the time during a blizzard?"

"I've read every book in the house three times and started erasing my crossword puzzles and filling them in again."

"All I do is make quilts. If we have any more blizzards, I'll have enough for everybody in the county."

"It's tough, but we've been through worse. Things will get better."

"That's for sure."

While the women are getting groceries, the men head for the local cafe. After seven no-school days, the kids are driving them nuts and they need some man talk.

"I haven't seen this much snow since the blizzard of 19__ (fill in the blank). There was so much snow it covered our two-story house and the neighbors had to come over and dig us out so we could climb out of the window in the upstairs bedroom."

"*The Farmers' Almanac* says we're going to have snow until April. In the Dakotas, we know that without reading it in *The Farmers' Almanac*."

"That snow is packed so hard, I've broken three shovels. What would we ever do without snowblowers? In some places the snow is too deep for the snowblower to cut through it."

"Better get our pumps fixed before the spring thaw. We're going to have basements full of water."

"You really think it's going to thaw?"

"Maybe by the Fourth of July."

"The deer are hungry. They've been eating the feed I put out for cattle."

"You're lucky if you can get your cattle fed. We're going to lose a lot of them this year."

"I feel sorry for the animals. It's a tragic situation."

"The sun came out yesterday. I thought I was in Florida."

"Did you say Florida? It's been cold there, too. Maybe we're better off right where we are. We've been through tough times before. We'll make it through this."

"That's for sure."

Poverty is a State of Mind

This has been a long winter, a long winter in which our spirits may have become impoverished with negative thoughts and conversations. How long has it been since we've heard someone exclaim over the beauty and delight of a snowfall? Probably at least four months ago when we were enjoying family gatherings at Thanksgiving time. In the midst of the miseries of shoveling snow drifts and chiseling ice from sidewalks and driveways, it's easy to miss the beauty of the full twilight moon as it swims in fluffy clouds which appear to be an extension of the snow on the horizon. And are we impressed with God's eye for fashion colors as he dresses the winter sunsets in shades of mauves, pale grays, and slate blues against the stark whiteness of the snow? It's easy to miss the richness of this God-given beauty as we struggle with the realities of elements beyond our control.

In many areas of our lives we can be as wealthy as our imaginations and our creativity allow us to be. Remember the old lament, "We're not poor, we just don't have any money?" How can we look wealthy or successful without spending a lot of money? Our family sometimes joked about looking good for nothing as we recycled ample yardages of fabrics from outdated adult clothing into frilly dresses for little girls or found a pair of perfect patent leather shoes for a dollar on a clearance table.

Since most of us don't have a lot of big things happen in our lives, we can learn to find pleasure in the small things of everyday living. A real treat can be something as simple as a cup of cappuccino for 89 cents at the local drive-inn. What a treat! And what a buy! This drink in the city could cost three times as much for half as much coffee. We can rejoice in ordering garden seeds and plants from the colorful seed catalogs. Just imagining how these hardy varieties of flowers and vegetables will look next summer is enough to lift the spirits.

We can learn a lot about enjoying the simple things of life by watching children. What a joy it is to give gifts to little ones before they become hooked into materialism. A two-year-old child is just as excited about receiving a 59-cent bubble pipe and bubble soap as a teenager is over getting a CD player complete with a speaker system.

We can learn to appreciate and enjoy some of the simple things we take for granted, such as visiting with a friend over tea, enjoying a beautifully written book, or eating popcorn and playing board games with family members.

We must have compassion and mission for the millions of people in the world who live in material poverty such that even their most basic needs aren't met.

But real poverty is in the mind of the person who has no hope, no imagination, no creativity, and no dreams.

It's Not As Bad As Last Year

Have we heard the phrase, "But you can be thankful it's not as bad as last year," enough times yet?

One November night I drove my forty miles to work with snow blowing around me and the sleet accumulating on the windshield so that the wipers couldn't keep up with it and I had to stop along the side of the road to scrape my windows so I could see. If I hadn't been following another driver's tail lights, I would not have made it to Aberdeen.

When I told somebody about it, he said, "But really you can't complain. You've had a good open winter for driving. It isn't as bad as it was last year."

One morning I drove home at 35 miles-per-hour maximum speed because of ice.

I shouldn't have told anyone about that because the remark was, "At least you weren't tunneling through a ten-foot snowdrift like you would have been last winter."

Then there was the morning in January when I tried to start my car after my ten-hour night shift at work and it was 31 degrees below zero. The car wouldn't start, I had to ask someone to hook up the battery charger, and my fingers were frostbitten because I took my clumsy mitten off when I put the key in the ignition and tried a dozen times to get the car started.

You guessed it. Someone said, "But it was worse last year." Never mind that my car was severely flooded, wouldn't produce enough heat to keep us warm, and my blistered hand felt like it was on fire.

Then there was the night that the snow was blowing just enough so that I had to drive with my lights on dim. Several times I met large trucks and found myself in total white outs. All I could do was slow down, keep the car pointed straight ahead, and pray.

Can we talk about the fog? Weeks of fog. Fog so thick at night that we couldn't see the signs along the road and the ground clouds kept coming in waves that made me feel motion sick.

Not seeing in '98 seems the same to me as not seeing in '97.

When my back ached from shoveling five inches of snow from the driveway, of course I was reminded that last winter I would have had five feet of snow to shovel. Never mind that if it had been five feet of snow, I'd have hired somebody to move it for me.

Well, folks, prepare yourselves to hear these types of conversations for the rest of your lives. Twenty-five years from now, no matter what you try to say about any particular bad winter day, someone sitting around the big table at the local cafe will say, "You think this is bad, Sonny. Hah! This is nothing compared to that winter back there in '96-'97. We had 108 inches of snow. Started in October, didn't quit till April. Snow up to the eave trough and we had a three-story house. You young guys nowadays don't know what 'tough' means."

So pick out your best Winter of '97 stories and polish them to perfection. You'll be using them again and again and again for a very long time.

Country-fied Spring

The Promise of Spring

It's March. Even though we've had a mild, open winter this year, I long for spring.

The house smells like it wants all the doors and windows thrown wide open for a thorough airing, but it's a bit too chilly yet. Plastic covers some of the windows and it's too soon to take it off because we will probably get at least one more blizzard.

I go downstairs to do laundry and follow a narrow path between piles of stuff that during the winter I thought I should save because it was too good to throw away and now it looks like garbage. I'll clean it out when the city sends trucks around for spring clean-up week.

I hesitate to clean the carpets or do too much scrubbing because the snow is still melting and mud is being tracked into the house no matter how careful we are to take off muddy shoes and boots at the door. If I clean now, I'll just have to do it again in another month.

The seed catalogs have been worn out with looking and dreaming and getting ideas for flower beds. I long for expanses of green grass to replace the drab grayness of winter and I hope to see bright tulips and daffodils early this spring.

I want to go for a walk without worrying about slipping, sliding, and falling on the ice. My muscles and joints ache from lack of exercise and too much sitting. They want the warmth of the sun to heal them. Perhaps I can even get rid of those few extra pounds I've put on this winter if I get out and do some physical work in the yard.

I look forward to seeing robins hopping on the lawn in their constant search for food and watching the V-shaped formations of geese flying north.

As I drive through the country, I'm eager to see little calves on wobbly legs trying to keep up with their mothers.

When I see farmers planting their crops, I am reminded of the faith they have that this year will be good. Their seeds will sprout and grow, there will be sufficient moisture, abundant yields, and a decent price for their grain.

What would we do without the promise of spring?

Spring Housecleaning

The snow is gone and the yard is showing the promise of green grass. The sun, shining for the first time in weeks, is energizing.

But alas! Those rays of the sun dancing through the picture window reveal dust particles that weren't noticed on cloudy days.

The bedroom that seemed cozy in the grayness of winter skies looks filthy in the harshness of daylight.

The lady of the house thinks, "This house looks like a pigsty. I can't stand it another minute. It has to be cleaned and cleaned right now!"

The windows are opened wide. "Out goes the bad air, in comes the good air!"

Everything is pulled out of the closets and dressers and put into piles–piles of things that can be used this summer, things to be packed away for next winter, things to recycle for quilts, things to throw away, things to give to someone smaller, or things to save for the grandchildren to remind them of their heritage.

Two conflicting cleaning philosophies come to mind. One is, "If in doubt, throw it out."

The other is "Better keep it. You never know when you might need it!"

Okay. Another pile is labeled "keep it for one more year and then make a decision."

The stale bedding is pulled off the bed and the dusty curtains come down to take their place in line beside the washer. The cobwebs are vacuumed off the walls and the bucket is filled with hot, sudsy water for a vigorous scrubbing. There's no rest until the carpet is shampooed and the woodwork oiled and shining.

The bathroom! Yikes! It's mission germ warfare. Lather the walls and tub surround with Pine Suds, disinfect the fixtures with chlorine bleach, and clean them with Lime Go. Disregard the warnings on the labels concerning mixing these household cleaners. If there's an explosion the pipes will be clean when they go through the roof.

It's late in the day, but there's no stopping now. On to the kitchen with the cleaning supplies.

The kitchen cupboards are filled with clutter that needs to be pulled out so shelves can be scrubbed and lined with colorful contact paper. Dishes that haven't been used in months are washed in hot suds and sterilized with boiling water. Drawers are emptied onto the table and the contents sorted into use, don't use but want to keep, and throw away. Why did anyone save three broken rubber bands, a package of yeast labeled 1989, a brown hair net, six rusty jar lids and a package of screws that look like they belong to something important, but who knows what?

In the midst of these piles, the lady of the house sits down with a cup of coffee to sort out the junk mail from the good mail.

Sitting down is her big mistake. She is too weary to get up again and says, "The rest of the kitchen cleaning will have to wait until tomorrow. Maybe I can skip the living room this spring. I did a thorough job on that last fall."

She pours herself another cup of coffee, puts her feet up on an overturned clothes basket, and reaches for the latest copy of Martha Stewart's *Living* magazine.

Guilt - It's My Job

I live in the Midwest, I'm a Lutheran, I'm the oldest "child" in my family, I was married, and I'm a mother.

Any one of these roles carries a heavy burden of responsibility and guilt.

In the rural Midwest, worth equals work. If I'm not working, I'm not worthy. I have a long list of shoulds each day and if those shoulds aren't done, guilt overwhelms me. I should give more to church, I should collect for the cancer drive, I am responsible for the well-being and happiness of my whole family, and everything my children do or don't do is my fault.

I can expand this realm of guilt to unlimited proportions. I can convince myself that slavery was my fault, that Oriental sweatshops are my fault, that if I earned more money, I could feed all of the hungry children in Central America. Guilt is a tough job but I've practiced until I'm good at it.

Two years ago for Christmas my daughter, Connie, bought me the whole gamut of quilting supplies–the cutting mat, rotary cutter, and an assortment of rulers and quilting books. I loved that gift and was so thankful to get something I wanted but would never have bought for myself without feeling guilty.

Then I picked up on what she was really trying to tell me, that she was learning how to quilt and would like to have those supplies for herself. So the next Christmas I bought her the cutting mat, rotary cutter, and an assortment of rulers and quilting books.

We both had something we wanted and weren't obliged to feel any guilt over having it because, after all, we had each done something nice for someone else, and that's okay.

When Connie called to wish me a happy Easter she said, "I've had my forty days of guilt." I asked her to explain that. She said, "From the time I was little, I thought that if I had been a good girl, Jesus wouldn't have needed to die. All my life, every year during Lent I have become that bad little girl again." What a burden!

In the church we have forty days of Lent and seven Sundays of Easter. It seems that we dwell more on death than we do on life. Guilt is easier than grace.

As we celebrate the seven Sundays of Easter, let's remember that we are Easter people. We are forgiven.

The death of Jesus frees us from sin and guilt and we live in the assurance of the resurrection.

Wandering in the Wilderness

The Israelites wandered needlessly in the desert for 40 years on a trip that should have taken them about eleven days from bondage into the Promised Land. Their whining and complaining and lack of faith in God's provision kept them from receiving the joy and peace they should have had.

We, too, have times in our lives when we wander in the wilderness. Everything is dry and empty. We feel a deep, deep sadness for all of the misery in the world.

We have things but no peace. We have money but no real love. We party and go to social events but have no meaningful, lasting friendships.

Sometimes the sadness comes as a result of events such as the loss of a job, loss of money invested, an accident which causes serious injury to someone we love, the death of a friend or a family member, the end of a relationship, or children in trouble. Problems with alcohol, drugs, or illnesses plague people we know and love.

What we get is not what we had planned for our lives. We don't know how to cope or where to turn for help. We are overwhelmed with decisions that have to be made yet we lack the ability or the motivation to make wise decisions.

Sometimes the sadness comes for no apparent reason and we don't understand the emptiness overwhelming us. We want to retreat and have time to search our souls, time to dream dreams, time to meditate and ask God for direction and comfort.

Even though we love people we want to be away from them for awhile but we have to make a living which means we have to work with or for people even when we would rather spend time alone. There is nowhere to go, nowhere to hide.

We work long, hard hours but have no satisfaction. None of our own input, our creativity, our individuality goes into our product or service. We follow directions of upper management, do as we are told, and work for a paycheck, only a paycheck. On the other hand, people in upper management can become discouraged as well when they have to deal with negative employees who work only for a paycheck and aren't willing to give a job their best.

We want to use our talents and abilities but we don't even know what those abilities are. Sometimes we doubt that we have any abilities and if we do acknowledge them, we don't know how to focus or direct them or use them in a career that will support a family. So we keep on with the job we have in order to provide, all the while feeling an emptiness deep-down within because we aren't using the talents we were given. We fail to make the choices that could alter our lives and make us happy, almost as if we fear success and happiness.

We look for something, anything, that will make us feel better such as prescription drugs, constant entertainment, miracle diets, mega-dose vitamins, magical natural dietary supplements, alcohol, food, or excessive work.

We pray, not to make it through the month or week or even the day, but for strength to make it from one hour to the next, to put one foot in front of the other a step at a time until inch by inch we walk through that valley of darkness, fear, uncertainty, and pain.

Having these thoughts and feelings doesn't mean we have lost our faith. It just means we are walking through a valley. We have the right to be down for awhile, to question, to wonder and wander, but after a time, we need to choose the joy God has for us right now. We don't need to wander for 40 years in the wilderness as the Israelites did.

Let's remember that we are Easter people. Even if we don't feel worthy of redemption we cling to the knowledge of the resurrection, the assurance of life, not just for the future, but for right now.

Eternity is now. Easter is forever.

Awesome!!

In days gone by, the word awesome was used to describe such natural phenomena as the Grand Canyon, Old Faithful or Niagara Falls. The Egyptian pyramids, the faces on Mount Rushmore or the Statue of Liberty, all carved or constructed with blood, sweat and tears of human labor, might also have been described as awesome. And certainly God was awesome.

However, the word awesome has lost its meaning. These are some examples of recent conversations I have heard.

"I got these gym shoes on sale for $125."

"Awesome!

"I bought this scientific calculator at the hardware store."

"Awesome!"

"I got a 92 in spelling today."

"Awesome!"

"Did you see Michael slam dunk that one?"

"Awesome!"

"That's an awesome haircut."

"They were handing out these awesome pens at the fair."

"AWESOME!!!!"

"NOT!!!!"

Winter is barren - empty - dead. Sometimes it seems that the only awesome thing about winter in the Dakotas is the fact that people survive it. And then the miracle happens. The sun shines warmly again. Chickens hatch, baby calves are born, the tulips pop through the soil and the grass which was dead starts to grow, the Easter lily blooms. What joy!

During the Lenten season, Christians throughout the world follow the journey of Jesus to the cross. Jesus knew what He had to do, but in his humanness He prayed in the Garden of Gethsemane that He would not have to endure such suffering. When He was sure of God's will, He obeyed without resistance, in order that the scriptures might be fulfilled. He could have come down from the cross and saved Himself but He chose instead to die for the sins of all believers.

"He could have called ten thousand angels, to destroy the world and set Him free. He could have called ten thousand angels, but He died alone for you and me."

But we dare not leave Jesus at the cross.

Dead.

Or in the tomb.

Buried.

For on the third day, He rose again. What a miracle! How can the human mind begin to comprehend it? The tomb is empty, praise be to God. Christ the Lord is risen again. Alleluia. The old familiar Easter hymns tell the story anew every spring. Life is reborn. That which was once dead is now alive.

Christians throughout the centuries have clung to this knowledge, the knowledge that if we are in Him, dying like Him, we shall also rise like Him.

AWESOME????

YES!!!!

Country Roots Grow Deep

After six months of unending, snowy whiteness I'm excited to see green grass, tulips ready to bloom, and peonies who valiantly triumphed over the harsh winter blizzards.

The poor weeping willow tree looks as though she has had a bad hair day. The deer, standing on ten-foot snow drifts, nibbled her top branches and I just finished sawing off the dead limbs. But to me, she looks beautiful, a symbol of survival in a harsh climate.

I sprayed my dandelions, and they look just as healthy now as they did before. Perhaps we should select the dandelion as the official state flower, cultivate soil for them, plant them in nice straight rows, fertilize them, weed them, water them, harvest their seed for sale, pay $14 per bushel for the greens, give dandelion arrangement lessons at every craft store in the Dakotas, and let the Environmental Protection Agency declare them an endangered species. They'd become extinct within three years.

As I'm spading one of my flower beds, my friend comes over and says to me, "You are working so hard."

I say, "How can you call this work when I love doing it so much?" She was raised in the city. She doesn't understand.

Spading, hoeing, planting. Those chores are my relaxation after a full day of doing my inside, sit-down jobs. I work at a leisurely pace, occasionally stopping to look at the pillow clouds in the blue sky and the robin nearby tugging mightily at an earthworm.

The garden fork turns over a clump of black earth from which I extract creeping jenny roots and I see new beginnings not only for my plants, but also for my future. Sometimes I find answers to life's probing questions in the wonder of the perennials growing steadfastly year after year. Even though no one does anything in particular for them, they just keep on blooming where they were planted.

I gaze at the container of pink and lavendar petunias my friend gave me and decide to put them in my horseshoe-shaped flower bed. They are blooming luxuriously now and the persistent petunias will bloom until the first hard freeze in the fall. I plant my 36 marigolds that I started in the house in February. They will form a vibrant border for my vegetable garden and their unpleasant scent will help deter some unwanted pests.

After that bed is planted, I reward myself with a cup of amaretto flavored coffee. While I drink my coffee, I plan the next flower garden or decide how much more of my yard to spade this year. Life doesn't get any better than this.

I return to my digging. By this time I smell like the earth. There is dirt under my polished fingernails, and mud on the knees of my jeans. The wind tousles my sun-dried hair and I am reminded that the wind was here before I was and it will continue to be here after I am gone, a power beyond my control. It helps me to put my small troubles into perspective, to remember the greatness of the One who created all things.

I realize that my roots are hopelessly entangled with the roots of the dandelions and crabgrass and I'm reminded anew that all life comes from the earth and returns to the earth.

And life in between the beginning and the end is lived one shovelful at a time. In memory of the past, life becomes nostalgically better than it really was. Each part of life was a struggle and had heartaches combined with the good times. If I try to look at what's ahead, try to see the whole picture, I see too many shovelfuls and I may become discouraged and give up.

All I really have is today, and that shovelful is enough.

A Tribute to My Mother

Many times throughout the year I think of my mother, but I think of her especially during May, the month in which we honor mothers.

As a child, I took her for granted as children will do, but at some point, probably when I had children of my own, I realized what a wonderful role model she was for us.

For the first fifteen years of my life I lived West River, thirty miles from Pierre, in a three-room house. It's amazing that such a small house could hold so much love and so many good memories. My family was a traditional family with Dad the financial provider, a take-charge kind of guy, and Mother the housewife as she was called in those days. If she ever felt unfulfilled in her role, she was a great pretender.

My mother was a multi-talented lady. She was a shepherdess, a farmer/rancher's wife, a wonderful cook, a dedicated mother, and a 4-H leader. If there was a church or community activity, she was there helping in her quiet, unpretentious way, wherever help was needed. When I look back at how Dad supported her in any activities of her own choosing, I think she was truly liberated.

Mother's hands were tough and calloused from the hard work of the prairie yet soft and gentle when she tucked us in at night and listened to our prayers.

She ordered Sunday School at Home lessons and read to us if we were homebound because of rain which made the gumbo road impassable or if the the snowplow was unable to plow us out for a few weeks in the wintertime. On those special Sunday evenings she cooked a batch of fudge and made a dishpan full of popcorn. In the wintertime we made ice-cream in a hand-cranked freezer. It had to be made with real cream and real vanilla.

We sat around the coal stove under quilts to keep us warm while our teeth chattered from the delicious coldness.

Housecleaning was not a priority for Mother. She often said, "I find more interesting things to do with my time than clean house."

In the middle of a mess, she would say, "Kids, put the fish poles in the pickup and let's go catch us a little fish for our supper."

She often said, "I'm happiest when my children are all home. They have too much school. They need more family time."

Imagine that!

Birthday cakes were always angel food and the birthday child didn't have to do dishes. It doesn't take much to make a child feel special and to make a memory.

Mother gave us the gifts of fun and music and laughter. If we weren't able to go to a dance, we danced in the kitchen. If we couldn't go to town on Saturday to buy paper dolls, we cut them out of an old Sears catalog. If we complained about being bored, she handed us a bucket of peas to shell or a broom for sweeping the floor. We became creative in finding our own ways to keep busy.

The gift of hospitality came naturally for Mother. There was always room for one more plate on the table, room for one more child to stay overnight, room for one more person to ride along on our way to somewhere. If each of my two sisters, my brother, and I invited a friend to go along, we had ten people in the car. What fun that was!

I think of her when I see a rainbow or a spectacular show of northern lights. She made a big deal out of beauty in nature. She would say, "Kids, come quick!" and as we hurried to see what she was excited about, she exclaimed, "Look at God's beautiful rainbow. Do you really think there's a pot of gold at the end of it?"

I sometimes thought, "A rainbow? Big deal! You called us out here to look at that?" Now I appreciate the rainbows in my life.

Mother practiced the fine art of detachment before it was given a name or became a "parenting skill." If we were all fighting over the sewing machine and begging for help with our projects she went out to the garden or the barn and let us figure things out for ourselves.

She said things which, according to modern-day child psychologists, destroy children's self-concepts and do permanent damage to impressionable psyches. Mother didn't know what "positive self-image" meant, she just wanted her children to behave themselves.

She said such things as, "If you kids don't quit fighting in the back seat, you're ALL going to stay in the car when we get to town."

"Behave yourself or you'll eat your supper standing up." (I don't remember ever getting a spanking. Apparently the threat was sufficient.)

"You should be ashamed of yourself for talking like that about your friend."

"Pretty is as pretty does."

When I sewed a denim jacket and one side of the collar was a half-inch longer than the other side, she said, "That looks terrible. You have to do it over again until you get it right."

I threw the jacket in the corner and said, "I'm not ripping it out," but a week later I retrieved it, did it right and felt proud to wear it with a perfect collar. I doubt that Mother thought then that I would become a professional seamstress!

Years later when I told her about how naughty and disrespectful I had been to her, she said, "I don't remember that."

She graciously developed a selective memory.

My mother has been dead for several years but I still want to call her to talk things over or to ask her opinion on decisions I need to make. I want to ask her how she froze the corn that tasted like fresh-from-the-garden corn in January or how she made the boiled butterscotch frosting so it didn't sugar. When I'm sick in bed, I wish she could come and make me a cup of hot tea and a slice of toast and touch my forehead to make me feel better like she did when I was a child.

I once said to her, "Mother, you've done so much for me, how can I ever repay you?"

She said, "Of course you can never repay me. Children aren't supposed to repay their parents. Just pass it on to the next generation."

"Okay, Mom. I'll do my best."

Graduation - The Beginning and the End

Students look forward in great anticipation to graduation, to what comes next, to "getting out of here and getting on with life."

That's the way it should be as they mature and prepare themselves for the next stage of their lives whether that stage is further education or entering the working world.

And yet a couple of years down the road, those same students are invariably saying, "I wish I had studied more. I should have listened to what my teachers were trying to tell me. I never had it so good as when I was in school."

When I graduated from high school, I thought I was really smart. When I graduated from college (a long time ago), I thought I was even smarter. Then I stepped into the working world, the "real world," and quickly realized how little I really knew. No amount of formal education prepares us for the reality of a job in which we have to produce constantly and consistently for eight hours every day, week after week.

A college degree doesn't necessarily guarantee us a job in the field of our choice. It doesn't guarantee us wealth, success, joy, or wisdom.

My mother's formal education ended after 8th grade but she had a doctor's degree in wisdom. She had the gifts of spiritual peace, an unconditional acceptance of people, and a love of learning. She often said, "I got my education in the school of hard knocks."

Experience is a great teacher.

Children are born curious. Just watching a small person makes me tired. An 18-month-old child has his motor running every waking hour while he checks out everything in his environment. He wants to know what makes things tick. That curiosity and desire to know should be a life-long process for everyone, not something that's "done" at graduation.

Obviously I think education is important but sometimes I think the more I study the less I know. Or stated in another way, the more I study, the more I know that I don't know.

After being in the work force for many years while raising a family and playing at being a responsible adult, I went back to school. I'm still curious. I want to learn new things. I want to try to keep up with some of the changes that are taking place in the world. When I get my next degree, when I "graduate" again, I won't think I'm quite so smart.

Learning doesn't prepare us for life, learning *is* life.

Playing Solitaire

The nest is empty. I alternate between dancing for joy on the ceiling and huddling under my fuzzy blue blanket in fits of depression.

My body hasn't adjusted to the possibility of eight hours of uninterrupted sleep. I still listen for a car in the driveway, a key in the lock, and a "Hi, Mom, I'm home. What's to eat?"

I shout, "Turn the radio down!" and I'm the only one home.

The phone rings and I call, "I'll get it!"

I've carried two ten-dollar bills around in my purse for three weeks. There must be a hungry teenage boy who wants one of them.

I can't just sit here on the couch. There must be someone or something that needs my attention.

I don't have to endure one more episode of *Married with Children* or *Monday Night Wrestling*.

It takes me five minutes to wash a day's dishes, half an hour to dust and vacuum, ten minutes to toss the load of clothes in the washer and another ten to put them away. What do I do with the rest of Saturday? I'd almost pay someone to drop some soggy towels and wet washcloths on the bathroom floor for me to step on.

The toilet seat stays put–no surprises in the middle of the night.

I have watermelon, green olives, and pretzels for breakfast. Who's to know? At suppertime I eat the pasta salad right out of the mixing bowl-with the mixing spoon. How do I fry one piece of chicken? If I make a beef roast, I have to eat roast beef for four days in a row.

Why do I have sunflower seeds and two 12-packs of Mello Yello in my grocery cart? I don't even like sunflower seeds and Mello Yello.

If having so much freedom is so wonderful, why do I feel so empty inside?

Guess I'll play another game of solitaire.

Red ten on a black jack. Black seven on a red eight. Two of hearts on the ace of hearts.

Sadie Plants Again

It happens every May, the day after Memorial Day. Sadie goes berserk.

She dashes, garden fork in hand, from one corner of her yard to another. She digs a flower bed here, a vegetable garden there. She plants petunias along the curb, 4-o'clocks along the driveway. She digs a square garden for marigolds, the California giants in the middle, surrounded by increasingly shorter marigolds. The row of caster beans will make a nice background for the perennial beds, and the circular bed is filled with irises, peonies, bleeding hearts, salvia, phlox, and zinnias which Sadie's mother called Joseph's-coat-of-many-colors. There are impatiens and pansies on the north side of the house where they will be protected from the hot sun. This year's experiment garden contains cleome, ranunculus, and amaranthus. They all look so pretty in *The Gardener's Delight*. And dahlias. For Sadie, dahlias are always an experiment because they never seem to have quite enough time to grow and bloom in the short Dakota summers. There is a petunia bed, V-shaped, right in the middle of the backyard. Oh, faithful, trustworthy, dependable petunias, the first flowers to bloom in the spring, the last to die in the fall. She plants her vegetables in nice straight rows. It's more practical to pick vegetables from nice straight rows.

Along about three o'clock in the afternoon, Sadie's son wanders out to inquire as to the possibility of having dinner. He can tell from the look in his mother's eye that dinner is not on her agenda today. As he looks at the mounds of dirt and the cartons of plants still waiting in line, he comments, "Keep digging, Mom. If you dig enough, I won't have to mow the lawn at all this summer."

He wanders back into the house for a peanut butter sandwich, a quart of milk, and a bag of nacho chips.

Sadie muses to herself, nobody else will listen, as she plants and digs. "Homer always says, 'Plant your potatoes on Good Friday, and you'll have all the potatoes you can eat next winter,' but what does he know? I always plant everything the day after Memorial Day. There isn't any frost and the ground is warmer then. Everything pops right out of the ground overnight. The year I had back surgery I planted all of my garden on June 10th. Best garden I ever had."

Hours later, Sadie looks at her watch and exclaims, It's already 10 p.m. My how time flies when you're having fun!"

Her nose is sunburnèd, her fingernails are all broken, her hair is like straw and her deodorant expired four hours ago. The moon is shining as she lifts a huge tub of fern and geraniums onto her deck. She stands up as straight as it's possible for her to stand. Those muscles will ache tomorrow.

She looks at the yard, misty green in the moonlight and says to herself, "Ah, yes! It feels good to work so hard. We'll have vegetables this fall and winter. And lovely flowers to look at. People need food for the soul as well as food for the body."

All summer long, Sadie works in her gardens. When she is upset, she chops weeds. When she is lonely, she talks to her rose bushes. And she works.

By the middle of July, her enthusiasm begins to wane as she picks pail after pail of green beans. She always forgets that a couple of packets of green beans would be enough. A half a pound she planted! Who would have guessed that they would produce so profusely? In the summer sun, she is sweating, swatting mosquitoes and being bitten by horse flies. She seems to be muttering something that sounds like, "Why was I so crazy?"

By the middle of August, she has used every recipe she has for zucchini. She has made zucchini bread, zucchini cookies, zucchini hot dishes, zucchini salad, deep-fried zucchini and even one zucchini mock-apple pie. Her family won't eat anything new because it just might have some of that green stuff in it. Her neighbors won't come to the door when she knocks. She might have another zucchini behind her back. She says to herself, nobody else is listening, "Remember, Sadie, you only need two zucchini plants. Repeat after me. 'TWO!' But no, you had to plant 12 feet of them."

By the end of August, when the tomato vines have sprawled over 75 percent of the backyard, Sadie moans, "Whatever possessed me to plant 48 tomato plants? A dozen would have been too many!"

By the middle of September after the 77th jar of tomato juice is aligned prim and proper behind the jars of whole tomatoes, stewed tomatoes, tomato sauce, tomato puree, and jars of salsa made from the home economist's new recipe, Sadie is praying for frost. She swears she will not be responsible for her actions if Homer says one more time, "It will all taste good next winter, Sadie."

So it goes every year. By January Sadie has forgotten last summer's madness, the sweating, the aching muscles, the callouses on her hands. When the seed catalogs come out and the snow is four feet deep, she curls up on her couch under her ripple-crocheted afghan. As she basks in the warmth of the fireplace, she fills out her order for seeds and bulbs and a couple of new exotic flowering plants. She landscapes her yard with colored pencils on graph paper.

And next year, the day after Memorial Day, unless it rains, Sadie will plant again.

Country-fied Summer

Shoulds for Dad

June is the month in which we honor fathers and think about the influence, positive or negative, that they have on their children.

There are some basic things that a "good Dad" does for his children.

A good Dad commands respect and obedience from his children without being verbally or physically abusive.

Dad should compliment his children when they've done a good job and he's proud of them. He realizes they need positive encouragement and that honest praise does not make them egotistical.

He lets children make their own decisions in areas appropriate for their age. He knows that sometimes the best lessons are those learned from making mistakes. He gives them room to explore their own interests, even though those interests may differ significantly from his own.

Dad is supposed to provide for his children's needs not cater to their every want and whim. (Well, okay. An occasional night out for pizza or a special pair of ice skates under the Christmas tree are permissible!)

Dad should get down on the floor to give horsey rides or play marbles with the kids.

Dad is supposed to support his wife in matters of discipline and granting permission. If children play the Mom against Dad game, Dad should say, "What did your mother say about this? You must listen to your mother."

He also says, "Whose turn is it to help Mother with dishes?" and he takes his turn with household chores from time to time.

A good Dad protects his children from the evils and dangers of the world until they are old enough to protect themselves. To the best of his ability, he sees that they live in peace, security, and safety and he prohibits them from doing things that are harmful to themselves or others. It is important for Dad to give his children moral and ethical standards to live by, not only in words and commands, but also by his lifestyle example. He works hard for a living, pays his bills on time, keeps his promises, and helps his neighbors.

He's big enough to admit it when he makes a mistake and apologizes for it. After all, children aren't perfect. Neither can they expect their Dad to be perfect.

He isn't ashamed to cry when sad things happen, and to show love in words and actions.

One of the most important things a Dad can do for his children is to take them to church with him. They need faith and the knowledge that there is a power greater than they are. They need the fellowship of others who care about them.

I once said to my Dad, "I realize more and more that many children grow up in abusive situations and live in neglect. How could I have been so fortunate as to have had parents who loved and wanted me?"

He said, "We only did what we were supposed to do."

I said, "Thanks, Dad, for doing what you were supposed to do!"

Life Is Lived One Iris at a Time

What a pitiful, depressing sight! The flower garden that I so enthusiastically planted and tenderly watered a month ago is overgrown with weeds so tall I can't see the pink cascade petunias and the dusty miller is choking in the clutches of the tenacious creeping jenny.

I think, "I can't face this formidable task. It will take me an entire day to weed this one little flower bed."

I start pulling up every deeply-rooted stem of crabgrass and separating every clinging weed from the long-bladed leaves of one iris until it stands alone, proud, tall, and weed-free.

"Now that wasn't so bad. I think I can do one more iris."

I do one more, then another and another, concentrating on only one at a time, not looking ahead to see how many dozens I have left to do. Once in awhile I stand up to examine the row I have finished and marvel at the pale green of the leaves against the background of the rich black earth.

My life is filled with a long list of so many things to do and so little time in which to accomplish them all. If I look at the big picture, I'm beat before I start. Maybe I can apply the iris theory to other areas of my life.

What about that dress and jacket that I cut out to sew for myself a month ago? I packed it away because I didn't have a whole day for working on it. What if I left it out and sewed one seam each day? It might take me a month, but so what? I would eventually have a new outfit to wear.

Then I have articles to write. I need an uninterrupted, stress-free block of time for the words to flow freely and naturally, and for the intense concentration of proofreading and rewriting so that every word is the best possible choice.

Sometimes I can't find that block of time, but I can write a few words or sentences while I'm cooking supper. I can jot down an idea while I'm going for a walk, working in my sewing room, or taking a break at work. After all, a story is written one word at a time.

What about the weeks when everything goes wrong? The kitchen plumbing springs a leak, the car has a temper tantrum and makes strange noises, a machine goes down at work and I don't get the overtime I had counted on, a family member has another crisis, I burn the hotdish I make for potluck, and I cut three blocks of a quilt the wrong size and have no more fabric for recutting.

If I allow myself to make long lists of the small, or not so small, crisis events of the week life seems so hopeless I want to hide out in a cave somewhere.

But let me apply the iris theory to this set of problems. I can turn off the water in the kitchen and carry water from the bathroom sink until the kitchen sink is fixed. I can take the car in tomorrow and if the mechanic can't fix it right away, I can either take a vacation day at work or borrow a car. I can't control the machines at work, but I can rearrange my bill paying dates. They will get paid.

I can listen to someone for a few minutes. That's all it takes, just a few minutes of listening. They don't expect me to solve their problems. I can pick up some fresh fruit at the store for the potluck. It's healthier and no doubt tastes better than my hotdish anyway. As for the quilt blocks, I'll just get creative and cut blocks of a contrasting color and tell people that's the way I planned it.

Let me remember that this problem solving doesn't all have to be done in one day. Some crisis situations become non-crisis situations if I wait awhile.

Now that wasn't so bad, was it? I think I'll use the iris theory more often.

Class Reunion Time

"Time has been kind to some of us and not so kind to some of us," one of my former classmates remarked at a recent class reunion.

I laughed at his remark then, but I've thought a lot about that since then. When we left high school, we had dreams, plans, goals, and visions for our futures. For many of us, God had other plans.

If we wander from table to table at an all-school reunion we can pinpoint how long ago each class graduated by listening to the conversations.

At the ten-year table, people are showing pictures of their babies, all beautiful, adorable, smart and perfect, of course. They are talking about the great jobs they have, the salaries that are buying them things they love, and the new homes they are building.

The guys are still young enough to be talking about what kind of trucks they own, how much beer they can drink without falling down, and, of course, babes.

Not everything in their lives is wonderful but they don't talk about those things. They put on smiles and join the conversations, pretending that their lives are terrific.

The 25-year people have developed a sense of humor. They joke about the age of 40 being over the hill, but they still feel the same inside as they did 25 years ago.

A few people bring out pictures of grandbabies, beautiful, adorable, smart and perfect, of course.

The most handsome boy in the class is now bald and looks just like his father.

"Could that be Mary, the plain girl nobody dated in high school? She's stunning, and she doesn't look a day over twenty."

After 25 years, people forgive some of the foolishness, embarrassment, and teasing that were endured as teenagers, and ask forgiveness for some of the mean things they did to others.

The people at the 40-year table have had a wealth of life experiences to share with one another. They no longer feel the need to impress anyone else so they can talk about their failures now as well as their successes. They realize that some dreams and goals are never going to be achieved, but most of them seem to have accepted their circumstances.

Some of them have set new goals and are working to better themselves or to use their talents for improving the lives of others.

They weep this year over the death of a classmate. He was much too young to die, and he had so much to offer the world. On the other hand, they are thankful for the one who had a mastectomy and now has no sign of cancer. She was the most beautiful girl in their class, but this year life itself is much more important than physical appearances.

"Can you think of that?" another group is saying. "Fifty years already. Why it seems like only yesterday we graduated and here we are all old and gray."

They rejoice with whoever shows up and the conversation centers around the joys and fears of retirement.

Yes, now they are free to talk about the fears, the feelings of loneliness and loss of purpose with no family or job responsibilities.

They become nostalgic in reminiscing about their school days, remembering details that had been long forgotten. Time has changed their perspective and things seem to have been better in the old days.

They talk about still feeling young inside. Mentally and emotionally they are the same people as they were fifty years ago, but body parts are wearing out. Medicare and social security are hot topics.

This group laughs a lot. They are determined to enjoy this reunion to the fullest.

"You never know. It might be our last," they say as everyone hugs everyone else.

Class reunions are joyful times for many as they look forward to seeing former classmates. For others, the memories from their school days are too painful. The old familiar feelings surface, the feelings of rejection, inferiority, fear of failure or being ridiculed.

Unfortunately, they never come back.

Shopping for School Clothes

The time had arrived once again for the yearly August pilgrimage to the mall to shop for school clothes.

On the way to the mall, everyone talked excitedly about styles, what they liked or disliked, and what they wanted to buy with their clothing allowances.

Dad and Mama had learned years ago to let the kids make most of their own decisions about what to wear because if they didn't like something, it would hang in the closet, unworn. However, that didn't keep them from offering some opinions of their own. Mama said, "I don't like most of the styles this year. Skirts are either draped around the ankles or barely covering the necessities."

Dad said, "I prefer the former. Whatever happened to dress codes?"

Hayley rolled her eyes and said, "Oh, Dad! Dress codes went out a hundred years ago. I think some judge in New York declared them unconstitutional. You're so old-fashioned."

"Being old-fashioned is part of our job description," Mama said. Hayley rolled her eyes again.

"Now remember, Cora," Mama continued, "it's all right to spend a little more for quality. And Dan, be sure you keep some of your money for later. You might need something new in January. Clem, have you made a list of the things you need? Last year you didn't buy enough and I had to take you back to get things you really needed. Hayley, I really prefer that you don't buy neon colors. You'll be tired of them and begging for more money before the year is over. And anybody who buys shoes that look like Grandma's has to walk home."

At that comment, Dad saw Cora roll her eyes and he said, "Now, Mama, we agreed to let them make their own decisions about what to buy."

At a men's shop in the mall, Dan picked out two shirts in neon, one orange and one green. Then he got a buzz haircut and had his eyebrow pierced.

Cora couldn't decide between the black pants and the navy jeans. The jeans cost $10 more, so she took the black pants. The shirts she liked best were expensive. She decided to look at fabric. If she used the pattern she bought last year, she could make four shirts for the price of one. Shoes were the most expensive item on her list, but she could live without a name brand and she found a real deal in Costless.

Hayley ran wildly from one store to another. She bought the first fall jacket she liked with no regard for the price. When she went to another store, she saw one she liked better for half the price, so she returned her first purchase. She had to find Dad three times to ask him to carry her things to the van.

Clem bought himself one pair of jeans then wandered off to put quarters into the video games.

The family rested beside the waterfall while they waited half an hour for Cora.

Dan was disappointed that no one commented on his haircut or pierced eyebrow.

Dad asked Clem what he bought. Clem said, "I don't need anything. I can wear what I had last year."

When Cora arrived with her bags of fabric, she beamed, "I really did well. I have everything I need for the whole year and I have $50 left over."

Hayley screeched. "Fifty dollars left over? Can I borrow it? There's a couple pairs of shorts and some earrings I want."

Cora said emphatically, "No way!"

As they strolled to the van, Mama asked Dad what he had in his blue plastic bag. "I think this neon shirt will be good for fishing. So what did you buy?"

"I found a pair of sandals for next summer at Costless. And on the $2-a-yard table I found the perfect prints for my quilting projects. I spent $88, but look at it this way. I actually saved $132 because it's regularly $4.98 a yard."

Dad just smiled as he put the key in the ingnition and turned the radio up to cover the noise of the chatter in the back of the van.

Relaxing at the Lake

Dad and Mama were tired. They had been working hard all year with no vacation, very few days off, and lots of overtime. The kids were getting bored with summer and school was a few weeks away.

"What we need is a whole week to ourselves, just the two of us with our kids at the lake. We can relax, sit on the deck with our lemonade while we watch the kids swim, or listen to them without interruption. We can take some time to renew our own relationship, to refresh our minds and rest our bodies. We need to get everything back into perspective. You know we haven't spent enough time with our family and the kids will be grown and gone before we know it," mused Mama one evening after a hectic day at the office. "I can feel it already, the cool lake wind in my face as the boat skims over the water, the sand between my toes as we walk hand-in-hand on the beach. And do you remember how beautiful the sunsets were at the lake?"

"Yes," Dad agreed. "I could do with a little time off myself. I have been kind of crabby lately. I suppose you've noticed?"

Mama only smiled and started making mental lists of things she needed to pack and the things she needed to finish before they left. It was always a lot of work to pack up four kids and a husband for a vacation.

On the appointed Saturday, Dad, Mama, Dan, Cora, and the twins, Hayley and Clem, arrived at the lake by noon exactly as scheduled. Dad had stopped twenty miles back to pick up some fast food so Mama would have time to relax a bit before she had to cook supper. They ate their almost-cold Macburgers picnic style on the deck. The kids were eager to start exploring and Mama was eager to start cleaning out the cabin so she could relax in clean surroundings. Somehow she just couldn't relax if things were not clean and in order.

Dad said, "The rains have been good to the lawn! It's going to take me the rest of the day to mow. I'm sure glad I thought about bringing that leftover paint. The cabin is in bad need of a paint job."

Mama had just finished sweeping the loft and putting clean sheets on the beds when Great-uncle Joe and Great-aunt Myrtle pulled into the driveway.

"We were out for a drive today and thought you just might be coming this weekend. Since we haven't seen you all summer, we thought we'd take a little detour and spend some time with you and your family, get to know the kids before they grow up. They do grow up so fast, don't they?" said Great-aunt Myrtle.

Mama started a mental list of how much to cook for supper and who would sleep where now that there were two more people in the picture. She had supper on the table for eight people when Uncle George, Aunt Ava, and their three children appeared, ready for a week of relaxation and fun. "Imagine that!" exclaimed Uncle George. "We all picked the same week to use the cabin. We didn't know you had planned to be here this week. Oh, well, the more the merrier, they always say. We'll just have to make the best of it, water down the soup, as they say. No problem for us!"

So Mama watered down the soup, cut the sandwiches in half, and set the table for five more. The table was designed for ten people at the max, but the kids could squeeze together on the patio benches. No problem.

While Mama washed dishes, she mentally revised her lists of where everyone would sleep and what she would cook for Sunday's meals. She would have to go to the store at the resort to stock up on paper plates and extra food items. Feeding thirteen was not quite the same as feeding a family of six. "Oh, well. Somehow it will all work out," she thought to herself.

On Sunday evening just as everyone was getting up from the supper table, Mama's friend Danielle, a single parent, and her five children arrived. Mama thought to herself, "I vaguely remember saying something quite casually about the lake being a good place for her children to be for a week sometime. I didn't think this week would be the sometime. Oh, well. Somehow we'll find room for a few more."

She forced herself to greet Danielle enthusiastically and asked if they had eaten supper yet. "Yah, yesterday," was Danielle's flippant reply. So Mama cleared the table, opened some cans, and reheated some leftovers in the microwave.

"Thank God I remembered to bring the microwave. It's a lifesaver," thought Mama and she mentally re-revised her list of what to cook for the next day and wondered where everyone was going to sleep at night. Actually, she was beginning not to care.

At midnight, Mama made a trip through the cabin, checking to see that everybody was in and settled for the night. There were 19 people in a cabin designed for six. Every bed was occupied. People were sleeping in sleeping bags in the loft. The hide-a-bed contained three children sleeping vertically and one sleeping horizontally at the foot. Great-uncle Joe was snoring in the recliner and somebody was curled up in a comforter in front of the fireplace. Mama found everyone present and accounted for and, miracle of miracles, the bathroom was empty. She locked the door, ran the tub full of hot sudsy water and soaked while she did her nails and drank a huge glassful of iced tea without interruption.

And so the week went, Mama cooking, doing dishes, cleaning, and washing load after load of swimming suits, bedding, and towels while Dad worked in the yard. He worked alone while Great-uncle Joe and Uncle George visited as they relaxed in lounge chairs on the nicely mowed lawn. Dad didn't get too upset. He rationalized that Great-uncle Joe was getting up in years and Uncle George's back was acting up again. Uncle George had all he could do to get up off the chair and walk to the refrigerator for a beer. Dad certainly wouldn't feel right if he asked him to lend a hand with a paintbrush.

It was a good thing that Dan and Cora were old enough to entertain the younger children. Dan raced up and down the lake with one boat load of kids after another. The braver of them got on water skis while Dan was driving the boat, the more cautious of the crew tried it only with Cora at the wheel. So it all seemed to work out. Hayley dug angleworms and caught frogs for bait for fishing. She spent most of her time baiting hooks for everyone else because nobody else would pick up a worm. When she wasn't baiting fishhooks, she was chasing the boys with a snake. For some reason it gave her a wonderful feeling of power. Clem just kind of hung loose and quietly observed everything that everybody else was doing. He would have a lot to write about on his first day back at school when he had to write, "What I Did This Summer."

Nothing good can last forever and so it goes with vacations. This one, too, came to an end. On the way home Mama said, "I don't believe this has happened to me again."

She got out her pocket calculator. "Let me add this up," she said. "I cooked Saturday night, three meals a day from Sunday through Saturday, breakfast and dinner on Sunday. That's 24 meals, add eight days of afternoon snacks, that's 32, take that times 19 people. That is 608 meals. Subtract 24 because Danielle didn't come until Sunday evening. That's 584 meals I served. If I wanted to be a chef, I'd apply for a job at the Steak House and get paid for it. To say nothing of the laundry. We took only six towels and I've washed and dried them so many times I think they are worn out."

Dad said, "Honey, it's your own fault. You should learn to delegate, disappear at meal time, let somebody else take some responsibility."

Mama said, "I know, but I just can't seem to do that. After all, Danielle has a tough life. It's not her fault her husband ran off with another woman and left her to raise five children by herself. She needs a vacation once in awhile. And come to think of it, I didn't hear *you* asking anybody to help you with painting, mowing, raking, weeding, repairing the fence or grilling the meat." ,

"Yah, you're right. I'm exhausted. Next year let's sneak away during the night and rent a hotel suite in Las Vegas."

They both giggled. They'd had this conversation before.

On Monday morning Mama did something she had never ever done in her entire life. She called her boss, told him she was sick, and went back to bed.

Gather Ye Rosebuds While Ye May

Winter comes too soon in the Dakotas.

After looking at snow for seven months of the year, white is not our favorite color.

We work so hard every spring to have a couple of months of color in our yards. We look at our backyards and absorb green. We admire the dazzling brightness of yellow marigolds bobbing royally above their shorter neighbors. We inhale the fragrance of every peach-tinged tea rose and study the detailed face of each purple pansy. We marvel over Blue Boy petunias and the burgundy dahlias.

We let the hot breeze caress our faces and the sun bleach our hair.

We try to soak up enough warmth to hold in our memories throughout the winter and dare not complain or pray for cooler temperatures because that prayer might be answered in January with exceeding abundance.

We go away from phones, VCR's, TV's, and computers. We intentionally forget the radio with headphones so we can hear the rustling poplar leaves speaking to us.

In the early morning we linger in bed to listen to the plaintive yet soothing coo of the mourning dove.

We put the withered bouquet of stemless wildflowers into a bud vase and tell the small child they are beautiful.

We help a child build roads and fields and haul grain with miniature farm implements so we can sit in the sandbox and feel the cool sand run between our fingers.

We play lawn croquet with the kids so we can go barefoot and feel the moist morning grass between our toes.

We lazily cast for bass almost hoping they don't bite. We spread a cloth on the ground for a picnic lunch of balony sandwiches, potato chips, bananas and real lemonade like we had when we were kids.

If the kids whine, "I'm bored," we tell them, "Boring is good for you. It prepares you for most of your life."

In the cool of the evening we go for a long walk and listen to the frogs in the creek singing in harmony with the whispering willows. We hope for a little breeze to keep the mosquitoes away. We walk west in time to see the magenta sun sliding away earlier than we like as the cool dampness settles in for the night.

Winter comes too soon in the Dakotas.

Country-fied Philosophy

Someday I'm Gonna

Somehow earning a living gets in the way of our lives and we don't do the things we'd really like to do.

How many times do we hear comments such as these?

"Someday I'm gonna take the kids fishing, but this week-end I have to work overtime."

"Someday, when I retire, I'm gonna make a quilt for each of my grandchildren."

"My wife really likes to eat out. When the wheat is in the bin, we'll have to celebrate."

"Someday I'm gonna get all these photographs labeled and put into scrapbooks for each of my children. Maybe I'll wait until I get my computer then I can scan them and print enough for my nieces and nephews, too. Yes, that's what I'll do."

"After the kids are grown up, I'm gonna go back to school."

"I really should go for a walk every day and maybe go to exercise sessions to get myself back into shape. I should eat more fruits and vegetables, too."

"Next Christmas I'll write individual letters in longhand to everyone on my Christmas card list. It's so much nicer to get a personal note, but this year they'll have to settle for a form letter or none at all. I'm just too busy."

"I wonder if I could still play the trumpet. I was pretty good at it in high school. Someday I'm gonna get it out and see what I can do with it."

"I'd really like to take painting lessons. Maybe when the kids leave home I can use their room for a studio."

My good friends were "gonna go to Hawaii" when both of them retired. They retired, she had a stroke, and he died. Their someday never happened.

For at least the hundredth time I told my daughter, Connie, "I'm gonna write and publish a book. In fact, I have ideas for at least three books. I'll work on them when I get a computer so I can format them so they will be camera-ready."

Connie said, "You know, Mother, time is passing more quickly than we realize. Maybe you should be doing that now instead of just talking about it."

Last week UPS delivered my computer and all its related equipment.
I think my someday has arrived.

"Are You Saved?"

"How long have you known the Lord?" a casual acquaintance asked me.

The question caught me off-guard and I hestiated before I answered, "I grew up with Him."

She seemed somewhat disappointed with my answer, as if she were waiting for me to tell a dramatic story in which I could give an exact time and place in which I had found God.

I often thought, "I have no story, no testimony," as I listened to compelling stories from people who had been in the depths of depravity and were miraculously saved from their dire circumstances. Sometimes I wondered why God hadn't revealed Himself to me in such an exciting way.

One day it dawned on me that God didn't need to reveal Himself to me in a dramatic way. I was baptized in the Christian faith and grew up with the knowledge that my salvation is by grace through the birth, death, and resurrection of Jesus.

The fact that I am assured of my salvation doesn't mean that I am good. Far from it. In one sense, no one is good enough or worthy enough to deserve God's grace, and yet God must have found something in each of us that was worth His dying.

My finite mind has a limited understanding of the theological concepts involved in God sending His Son to earth to live and die for us but I claim the promise.

People in the upper Midwest are of predominantly German or Scandinavian descent. They don't talk a lot about their faith. They internalize their knowledge and don't often discuss their feelings with others. Their Christianity is such a part of their identity and their background that talk seems unnecessary. Their faith is more apt to be shown in good works – a benefit dinner for someone who has cancer, sharing farm work or equipment with a neighbor, stopping on the highway to help a young woman change a tire, making layettes for newborns, or sharing garden produce.

They believe that faith without works is dead. They feel uncomfortable when someone asks them, "Are you saved?"

Their first reaction is probably, "Saved from what?" or, "I was never lost."

They don't know how to answer the "Are you saved?" question. They don't have a dramatic testimonial.

Perhaps the works people need to start talking more about their faith and the "Are you saved?" people need to put more action into their faith. But then everybody would be the same and that would be boring. Maybe we just need to appreciate and respect the differences in people.

Everybody has a God story. Perhaps we can learn to listen to the God stories of others even if they tell it in a style different from our own.

Maybe we can find a balance in the faith or works concepts and acknowledge that each person's God story is valid. Maybe we can accept them and love them no matter which style of worship they choose.

Don't Hit

Two children fight over a toy. The little one hits the big one and grabs the toy. The big one hits harder and takes it back. Mother slaps them both and says, "Don't hit!"

The bully gets the sandbox and all the toys in it by kicking the other children and throwing sand in their faces.

Daddy hits Mama if he doesn't like the hamburgers she cooks for supper and she tries to "do better next time."

The good guys on TV get rid of the bad guys with guns which supposedly makes it okay since they are good guys.

Then we shake our heads and wonder why kids use violence to gain power and control, to get what they want in life, or to try to solve their problems.

I'm amazed when I hear people (often young children) say that they can watch shows containing gruesome fighting and gore because it doesn't affect them. If that is really true, something is very wrong with their sensibilities.

I believe that everything a person sees and hears affects that person in some way. It may not be a total recall, but it is there somewhere in the subconscious mind.

When I was in my early twenties, I saw a movie in which a woman chopped off her husband's hands and head. My word! I had nightmares about that show for three months afterward and I can recall nearly all of that movie to this day. Now children are seeing such grizzly shows as that on the TV screens in their living rooms on a daily basis. Can we begin to imagine what goes on in those children's minds?

I remember the first time that I became aware of what TV was doing to my daughter. She always woke up early on Saturday morning to watch her cartoons while I slept a little later than usual. I thought the cartoons were harmless entertainment until one Saturday when I found her crouching behind the couch in fear from what she was seeing. She was afraid to go near the TV to turn it off. Then I started watching more closely to see what she was watching and we made some different choices.

Young children can't tell real from pretend, or the pretend is so real that they have trouble distinguishing one from the other. After a steady diet of shootings and beatings in which they feel no pain, they become desensitized and don't think of it as being so bad.

Concern for the quality of the programs children watch is one major concern, but the quantity also needs to be limited in order to provide children the time to do creative things, read, do their chores or use their imaginations in play.

There are parents who allow their children only a small amount of TV per day and help them to make wise choices concerning what they watch. I'm not too worried about those children.

But thousands of children go home to an empty house after school or spend many unsupervised hours each day because both parents work, usually out of necessity. Those are the children for whom society needs to take some responsibility by cleaning up the prime time programming.

I wish our society could think more about what's good for us and for our children than to think merely of the bottom line – "How many millions will this movie or this program make?"

I wish that we could regulate ourselves without governmental controls.

I wish that each of us would take steps to minimize violence in our country. I wish.............

Be Still

"Be still, and know that I am God." Psalm 46:10

Noise, noise, noise.

Everywhere we go there is noise.

There is so much noise that we find ourselves constantly saying, "What's that? I can't hear you. You'll have to speak a little louder."

Yes, speak a little louder so we can hear above the noise.

There's no escaping it. We go shopping on a Sunday afternoon and have to endure the blast of surround sound from the loudspeakers in the mall.

We try to enjoy a live concert featuring talented musicians, but the volume is so high it actually hurts our ears and gives us a headache and we wish we had stayed home.

During a church service, if the pastor allows more than two minutes for silent prayer and meditation, the congregation grows restless.

We make a business phone call. The operator can't allow us even a few minutes of silence while we wait for the call to be directed. Canned music, usually bad canned music, assaults us even as we wait for our connection.

The minute we step into our houses after a stressful day of work we automatically hit the remote control to turn on something, anything, even though there's nothing good to hear. We can't bear the silence.

We try to fill any interval no matter how short with talking, with sound, any sound, to fill the emptiness.

We wonder if God were to speak audibly to us today, would we be able to hear Him above the noise?

In scripture, we read that Jesus went away to quiet places, a lake, a garden, to rest, to meditate, or to pray.

Can we, in the midst of our world of noise find times and places of silence and peace?

Where can we go to escape the noise of the world and quiet the noise within us?

Where can we find places that soothe and heal the soul? How about:

Walking alone on a prairie road where we hear only the grasshoppers in the hay field or the frogs in the nearby creek?

Camping beside a lake with the sound of waves breaking on the sandy beach or the distant cry of a loon.

Watching a sunrise from a backyard deck while a mourning dove serenades us.

Observing the miracles of perfectly formed tiger lilies and burgundy roses while working in our flower beds with no sounds except the buzzing of bees and the whispers of the maple leaves in the breeze.

"Be still and know that I am God."

I'll bet we can hear Him if we listen.

Dream Houses

The first page I turn to in the Sunday paper or in the *Farm Forum Supplement* is the floor plan.

I carefully study each plan and make mental revisions as to how I would build it if I had an unlimited budget. I clip out those that I really like and save them in my manilla folder labeled "Floor Plans I Like." Once every five years or so I clean it out and throw away those that no longer appeal to me as my lifestyle changes. I have done this since I was a child.

When I was a teenager I planned the dream house I would have when I married my rancher boyfriend. We would build a ranch house with a red brick exterior, a big picture window, and an attached garage with a concrete floor instead of having a shed with a dirt floor. When the kids caught fish in the dam, I would fry them in my U-shaped kitchen with the white metal cupboards and a red-tiled floor. We would have carpet in all the other rooms instead of old-fashioned linoleum.

I didn't marry my rancher boyfriend and I didn't take my kids fishing. So on to the next dream house.

How about a split-level with a foyer instead of a porch or entry way? A recreation room in the basement would be great for entertaining family and friends. The main floor could have the kitchen, formal living room and dining room, and the three bedrooms upstairs would feature spacious closets for all of the nice clothes my family and I would be able to buy on an unlimited budget.

Since I didn't have an unlimited budget, I bought furniture at moving sales or recovered an old chair or brightened up my life with a fresh coat of paint in the living room. But I never gave up my floor plan file.

When I go to a larger city, I like to drive around and look at houses. I usually do this only if I have my sister or a woman friend with me. They have vision and imagination. It's not much fun to look at houses with men. They are practical and say such stifling things as, "Keep everything in a straight line. You want a straight roof line. It's lots cheaper to build and they're not as apt to leak."

"There are too many big windows. You want the windows higher and smaller to keep the heat from escaping in the winter time."

"This plan is not practical. You'd have plumbing all over the house. You need to have it all in a central location. Put the bathroom back-to-back with the kitchen and have the utility room in the same area."

Never mind practical. I'll just keep on dreaming as though I have an unlimited budget. My next dream house will have a huge sewing room with plenty of windows on two sides. It will be big enough for cutting tables, a quilting machine, a felt-covered designing wall, and a big comfortable chair for relaxing while I do hand work. I will have a sunny nook with a desk for my computer and lots of book shelves and storage for my writing and reference materials. Since I don't like to cook, the kitchen can be small with an eating bar. The open living and dining area needs a fireplace and I'll want a small bedroom for myself and a spare room or two for company. My work rooms will have a view, either a lake or mountains and I'll enjoy the view from my screened-in porch or the terrace or the gazebo.

Okay. Back to reality. I'm contented and thankful for my little straight-line house with the plumbing in the middle. It has been good to me and my family.

But if I choose to retire here someday I could add a garage with a studio above it, an octagon-shaped sunroom off the kitchen, or a bay window in my bedroom. I could knock out the wall between my bathroom and my walk-in closet to make it roomier. I could move the basement stairway to make the dining area larger, I could..................

God with Skin On

Little Eddie was afraid of the dark so his mother tucked him in, read him his bedtime story, and tiptoed quietly out of his room. But in his fear, he imagined all sorts of monsters and dragons and bad guys coming to get him.

He cried out for his mother. When she went in to investigate, he said, "I'm scared by myself in the dark."

Mother said, "You don't have to be scared. Just remember that God is with you."

Eddie was not to be consoled. He said, "I need somebody with skin on."

It is difficult for us with our finite minds to grasp the fact that God sent His Son, the baby born in Bethlehem, a baby "with skin on."

God was sent in human form. God is Jesus, Jesus is God, so God sent Himself? He existed from the beginning, was with God at creation, yet was created anew as a man to walk on the earth among people, to work with them, to laugh with them, to teach them. He experienced all the emotions and temptations that humans experience, yet was made perfect, without sin. Who can comprehend this? God as man. What a concept! It's a concept to be accepted with faith, yet mortal minds struggle to understand the greatness of it.

Theologians and intellectuals have tried for centuries to explain how Jesus, fully God, fully man, came to earth for the redemption of human beings. Each of us in our humanness must wrestle with the questions we have.

How should Christians respond to the generosity of God? This is an individual question. Each of us comes to our understanding of God in unique ways. Each of us has a "God story," a story of how and why we came to our faith, or how and why we are still searching. Each of us also must decide how to respond to our faith by finding our own special niche in which to use our unique God-given talents and abilities for mission or ministry.

By faith we can remember what God did for us and reach out to others to represent "God with skin on."

Grief

A death in the family usually brings an immediate whirlwind of phone calls, cards, letters, visits, food brought in. People gather around the bereaved to express their care and concern in the only ways they can think of when there are no words to be found to help the pain go away.

People tend to want to make everything better right away, but in actuality, grieving takes a long time. The pain will lessen with time, but the emptiness remains. Three months, six months, or a year later, the family still needs to talk about the death, and true friends will be there to listen.

When my friend's father died, his mother seemed to handle the death, the funeral, and living by herself quite well. A year later he was stunned when his mother said, "Dad's really gone, isn't he?"

It took her a year to accept the reality of her husband's death.

Almost a year after my mother-in-law died of cancer, I heard my daughter screaming and sobbing in her room. When I asked her what was wrong, she said, "My Grandma's gone. She will never brush my hair again. And I'll never get to snip her quilt blocks apart as they come off her sewing machine."

When my mother died in January, I didn't cry at her funeral. In a way I had said good-by to her ten years prior to her death when her mind started slipping and she quit calling me on the phone or talking to people. She was not the mother I had known. The first time that I really cried for her was on Mother's Day when I woke up and thought, "I have no mother to buy a present for!"

For weeks after she died, whenever I drove away from Dad's house, I would automatically look back to see her wave at me from the window as she always did.

It was hard to go visit Dad at first. Her chair was empty. The head says, "She's in a better place. She's with the Jesus she loves and is reunited with her twin sister and her little boy," but the heart says, "I want her here to tell me one more time that she loves me."

The death of an older person, even though it's difficult to accept, doesn't come as a total shock as does the untimely death of a younger person.

One of my best friends, a kindred spirit, committed suicide over ten years ago and I still think of her and miss her desperately. I will never know why she did it and I will always wonder if there might have been something I could have done to prevent it. Sometimes I'm angry at her for denying me years of her friendship, but mostly I just miss her.

I lost another dear friend almost two years ago. Again, my head tells me she's making beautiful music with the angels in heaven, but I want to call her and ask her what color to paint my bedroom or which pattern to use for my crocheted tablecloth.

People grieve in different ways. Some go into a deep depression. Some grieve inwardly and everything seems all right on the surface. Some may vent their grief by slamming doors and throwing things, showing their anger at God for "taking" someone they loved, or anger at the person for "leaving." We never know how we will react to death ourselves and we should never be surprised at the way another person reacts.

Most people I've talked to who lose a spouse say, "The nights are the worst."

They stay up as long as they can and get up as early as possible to avoid the loneliness of the night. They often feel a presence in the room. Sometimes they sleep in a different room because it's too frightening to be where "someone is watching them."

Holidays with family gatherings are difficult after a death. Even though everyone tries to maintain the usual traditions, a cloud hangs over the festivities. A certain place at the table is empty, the pie crust isn't quite as tasty, the family jokes aren't as funny.

Platitudes don't help, but death is a part of life. Perhaps the best thing we can do for people is to listen to their stories as often as they need to tell them. If we are the ones who need consoling, the best thing we can do for ourselves is to find someone willing to listen to us.

Grow Old Gracefully, Or Consider the Alternative

One day it happens to all of us if we live long enough. We look in the mirror and see wrinkles, crow's feet at the corners of our eyes, and gray hair, or the thinning of it. We go to buy new clothes and have to admit that the relaxed fit jeans feel more comfortable than the classic cut, but we aren't quite ready to resign ourselves to the baggy design which would camouflage the rounded tummy. We used to be able to sleep until noon, but now the body aches if we stay in bed too long in the morning. We would rather listen to "Prairie Home Companion" than Hootie and the Blowfish.

Sometime during middle age, whatever that may be, we start to think about what we have accomplished with our lives and wonder if it's enough. We ask ourselves the question in Peggy Lee's song, "Is that all there is?"

If there is more for us to do with our lives, what should it be, and are we too old and set in our ways to make the necessary changes in our lifestyles?

We go out for dinner and the waitress asks us if we qualify for the senior citizen's discount. Whether we take that as a compliment or an insult reveals much about our own attitude toward aging and much about our society's attitude toward aging.

Oriental cultures and Native American cultures traditionally venerate their older people and have respect for the wisdom and experience which come with age. The American culture, on the other hand, is youth oriented. Televison commercials and programs, magazine ads, and clothing styles are focused on youth. Youth is to be emulated, age is to be feared, joked about, or put on hold, like Jack Benny's eternal age of 39.

If we are honest with ourselves, do we really want to stay young forever or do we embrace and enjoy the changes that come with the new decades of our lives?

Each age has problems, challenges, joys and responsibilities.

Many older people are as energetic and enthusiastic as younger people.

We may have even more fun because we no longer have to impress anyone else. We have become comfortable with who we are and define fun and fulfillment on our own terms, without worrying about what we "should" be doing.

An 85-year-old acquaintance said, "I thank God for every extra day He gives me. He promised us three score and ten years and He has already given me 15 years more than He promised."

What a wonderful attitude, an attitude of thankfulness and growing old gracefully.

The Love of Money

We often hear people say, "Money is the root of all evil," but the actual quote is, "The *love* of money is the root of all evils." (I Tim. 6:10)

Money is neither good nor evil. It has no value except the value given to it by people. It is after all, only a commodity, like a sack of potatoes or a bale of cotton. Money can be a blessing or a curse depending upon a person's attitude toward it, the love of it, and the methods used to obtain or accumulate it.

Money is such a difficult and touchy subject. In any organization, whether it be city council, church building committee, park and recreation board, women's guild, state and national government agencies, more disagreements arise over money (the lack thereof, the appropriation of funds, budget priorities) than all other topics combined.

Think of the families you know who have been torn apart or marriages broken up over disagreements concerning money.

People who are blessed with great riches may hang on tightly to their wealth for fear of losing it. Loving money and the material things it can buy above all things is a sin, which poor people are often quick to point out.

But think about this. The poor envy those who have money and think that if only they had a given number of dollars, their problems would all be solved. Envy and covetousness are also sins. That's a hard thing to admit.

Have we noticed that those who have not tend to ridicule or shun those who have?

What comments do we hear them make?

"We are poor and proud of it."

"He's just getting too big, but the bigger they are the harder they fall."

"I could be happy, too, if I had his money."

Wouldn't it be wonderful if everyone could rejoice with those who are successful in business?

What would communities do without the businesses which succeed?

Lots of money in the bank accounts of those people whose attitudes and actions are right concerning money is indeed a blessing to an entire community. Who else but those with discretionary income are going to donate to build hospitals, schools, or cultural centers, give to scholarships, mission work, shelters for the homeless, disease research, and the list could go on and on.

Look at the example of Job in the Old Testament. Everything he had, family, herds, riches, were taken from him and he sat mourning in a pile of ashes. Yet he did not curse God for his calamities.

After Job prayed for his friends, the Lord restored his fortunes two-fold and he had many happy days thereafter. God chose to reward Job's faithfulness with material things.

In the New Testament, we find more parables and teachings on money than any other subject. God knew how hard it would be for all of us to get our priorities right in regard to money, that we might use people in order to get money instead of using money to benefit people, or worse yet, that we might let money become our God.

Something to think about as we go about this week's business.

Paying for the Privilege of Being Single

Perhaps I'm getting overly sensitive about an issue that really isn't an issue at all. Call it a pet peeve, a minor annoyance, something that on a scale of 1 to 100 ranks about 101, but why do single people have to pay more?

Why does a "single ticket" to something, anything, cost more than a "couple ticket?" Perhaps you hadn't noticed, in which case, you are probably married.

If I go to a dance (which I did once or twice a couple of years ago) ticket prices read $3 for a single, $5 for a couple. Do I take more space on the dance floor because I'm single? Will I dance longer, therefore requiring the building to be heated for a longer period of time? Should I "couple up" with a single man at the door so we can each save fifty cents?

Concert tickets are advertised as $6 per person or $10 per couple. Does a couple see less or hear less than a single person?

When I read the information from the class reunion committee I note that I should enclose my check for $15 with my reservation for dinner and entertainment and a couple should send $25. Do I eat more because I'm single? Perhaps. After all, it's been awhile since I've been out and I'll have to make up for lost time. The next time I get this opportunity, I think I'll protest by sending a check for $12.50.

Country Club dues might be listed as $75 per single and $125 for a couple. I can't think of a reason for that unless the assumption might be that a single person has fewer responsibilities and therefore has more discretionary money to spend.

Perhaps there's more truth than fiction in the old adage that says, "Two can live as cheaply as one."

Rent or a home mortgage payment is the same whether one person lives in the home or a dozen people live there. A car payment of $200 a month costs a single person $200. If two people share the car, it costs $100 per person. Property taxes depend upon the value of the property, not upon how many people occupy the property so in fact, the single person pays a higher share.

As a single person, I have a certain amount of freedom and independence that some married couples do not. I can come and go as I please, eat supper whenever I'm hungry, read or write all night without interruption, buy what I want without asking someone's approval, or watch a whole TV show without someone channel surfing.

Perhaps in the final analysis, being single is worth a few more dollars.

Sweepstakes - Bane or Blessing?

Most of the people I know have joked about having all of their problems solved by winning the lottery.

I have to admit, I've thought about what I would do if Ed McMahon appeared on my doorstep with a real check for me for several million dollars from Publisher's Clearing House.

In my dreams I build a lake home, write a check for a little silver sports car right off the new-car lot, pay all my debts and buy five pairs of shoes all at once whether I need them or not. I'd probably buy a whole yard of each quilting fabric I like instead of one-fourth of a yard. Beyond that, I wonder.

Would I continue to shop at discount stores, clip coupons, comparison shop for the best buys on groceries and buy unpretentious, ordinary clothes?

Would I quit my job, give up my business, hire someone to do my cleaning, cooking, and yardwork?

How would my friends and relatives react? Would they be genuinely happy for me and rejoice in my good fortune or would they be jealous and resentful? Would they continue to treat me as the plain, ordinary country girl that I've always been?

How would casual acquaintances react? Would people I hardly know suddenly want to become my best friends?

Would my attitude toward life and other people change or would I still find joy in the simple pleasures of life as I always have?

Of course, I'd want to give some to worthy causes, but how would I determine who or what was worthy?

Would I save an endangered species, feed hungry people in an African village, build an inner-city school, start a business which would employ dozens of people?

I'll bet my mailbox would be full of cards and letters from people who thought they could be my worthy causes. My phone would be ringing off the wall with calls from telemarketers willing to help me with my financial planning and salespeople offering me the best deals of the twentieth century. The paparazzi would be dogging me for photographs and the tabloids would write ridiculous stories about what I did with my money.

Would I be harassed and threatened by con-artists who knew about my winnings? Just imagine! Members of my family could even be kidnapped and held hostage for ransom.

My goodness! My life could become terribly complicated. I'd probably have to change my name, move to a secluded, undisclosed location, have an unlisted phone number, gain fifty pounds, wear horn-rimmed sunglasses, dye my hair black and let it grow down to my waist.

The more I think about it, the more reluctant I become to send in my last-chance-to-win envelope with the silver car pasted in the black square, the gold star in the circle, and the NO box checked on the back of the envelope. The responsibility of being publicly wealthy would be more than I could handle.

Maybe I could pray that I would win one of the 5th prizes of $50,000. I think I could handle that amount. Perhaps I could invest it and become quietly wealthy, so no one would know.

Try Reverse Psychology

I sometimes wonder if we go at parenting with the wrong approach. We seem to emphasize the very choices we wish children not to make and attach great importance to the things we prefer them not to have or to do.

For example. When we set a plateful of nutritious food in front of a child we say, "Clean up your plate and then you can have a cookie."

Certainly we are in effect telling the child that a cookie is much more to be desired than the meat and veggies on the plate.

I suggest these alternative lines to use in training a child to eat healthy foods. It will take some practice, but I think the results will be worth the effort.

"Edith Anne, you have two cookies left on your tray. Eat up, girl, or you won't get any broccoli."

"Edgar Allen, get out of that refrigerator right now. Supper is almost ready and those carrots will spoil your cookies."

It would be my guess that cookies would soon lose their appeal and carrots and broccoli would be the mission of the week.

When Edith Anne throws a temper tantrum, encourage her to continue by demonstrating a few techniques of your own. Don't be surprised if she stops in mid-scream to observe in astonishment as you stamp your feet and pound the wall with your fists. If that doesn't do the trick, set the timer and tell her she has to kick and scream for twenty minutes without stopping. It works.

When Edgar Allen becomes a teenager and talks about getting a real short haircut as in, oh, gasp, shaving his head, refrain from screaming, "Shave your head? Have you lost your mind? You'll shave your head over my dead body, young man," which, of course makes such a haircut the most desirable haircut in the world.

Instead, greet his announcement with exuberant excitement and carry on in glowing terms such as, "Hey, a man's gotta do what a man's gotta do. I've always liked the looks of bald-headed men. You have a perfectly shaped head. Come to think of it, I have a pair of barber scissors and an electric clipper. I'll go get them. Let me save you a few dollars. I'll just finish it off with a couple of disposable razors. No problem."

Are you worried about teenage pregnancies and concerned that your children may acquire sexually trasmitted diseases? Insist on sex education in school, lots of it. Give them tons of workbook pages, vocabulary flash cards, units integrating sex into every subject area. It would be like geography classes. They would read about it, memorize for written tests, write fifteen page theme papers, but never go there. They would be so bored they wouldn't think about it until they were 21, perhaps not even then. We could ensure zero population growth within one generation.

Then, just for kicks put math equations and formulas into the computer, save them under secret passwords which only teachers and parents have. Let the kids know that under *no* circumstances are they to get into the math sections and if they should happen to stumble upon them by accident, they are to report to a teacher or parent immediately. They will have cracked the secret code by age eight and be miles ahead of the rest of the world in math knowledge and computation skills.

I'm sure you can come up with some creative ideas of your own. Even if they aren't practical it gives us something to laugh about and maybe that's the best parenting advice. Lighten up. Learn to laugh at ourselves and to laugh with our children. In a stress-filled world we need every laugh we can get.

Waste Not, Want Not

I woke up from a nightmare.

I dreamed the end times had come and I was standing before St. Peter. I wanted to go in to heaven but all the food I've thrown out in my lifetime was piled up in front of the Pearly Gates. He said, "Do you really think you deserve to go in?"

Holiday meals were always special in my family even in lean times. On the farm we grew or raised most of our food and Mother cooked the traditional foods to perfection, mashed potatoes with lots of cream, brown gravy, peas or green beans with cream, whipped jello with fruit cocktail, dill pickles and green olives that we bought only for special occasions, homemade apple or pumpkin pie, and ice cream made in the old-fashioned freezer that we all took turns cranking.

Even as a child at holiday meals, I thought about children who didn't have a mother who cooked such a bountiful meal when we had so much on the table and scraps left over that went into the slop pail for the chickens or the hogs. At least the leftovers weren't wasted then as the animals ate them.

Now the scraps go into the landfill or down the garbage disposal and I hardly feel a twinge of guilt.

Not that we need to feel guilt for having blessings and plenty of food on our tables. But we might consider what we can do to enable other people also to have blessings.

I'm often amazed at the quantities of food served when I'm eating out. What do I do when the waitress brings me an appetizer salad that covers a platter then enough meat and potatoes for two? Some restaurants offer children's meals or smaller portions for senior citizens. Why not offer smaller portions to everyone? They could still have the regular menu for those hard-working people who need more food.

World-wide, we don't really have a food production problem so much as we have a distribution problem. If we think about it, most households in America have enough food to feed another family. We eat too much and we waste too much.

Each of us must decide how we will contribute to the well-being of others. It might be through buying less in order to be able to give a donation to World Hunger, or giving to the local food pantry because there are people in our own state and county who are hungry. Perhaps some of us have the skills to educate people, to teach them how to grow and produce their own food. Perhaps it's such a simple thing as giving up one cup of coffee and piece of pie per day and putting that money in the benevolence envelope.

I hope that St. Peter will be able to balance my mountain of leftovers with enough giving, sharing, and responsible living at the end of my life.

Where There's a List There's Hope

Times were tough. We were out of bread. My daughter said, "Put bread on the list, Mom. Man doth not live by peanut butter alone."

I put bread on the list. The fact that I put bread on the list did not necessarily mean that we would buy bread today. But we would buy it tomorrow, maybe, if some money came in. As long as it was on the list, there was hope of getting it. To this day if we want something, whether we can afford it or not, we say, "It's on the list."

Where there's a list, there's hope. We will get it, if not today, then tomorrow or the next day or sometime.

I have lists for today, tomorrow, next week, next month, a year from now, five years from now. I make lists of books I want to read, books I have read, vacations I want to take, things I wish I had said, things I wish I hadn't said, things I need for my cabin (I don't have a cabin yet. It's on the list.), things I will do when I win the lottery.

I just made another list!

Things can be listed in so many exciting and challenging ways. Sometimes I prioritize. Sometimes I cut the list apart and make myself a job jar so I can surprise myself. Sometimes I list all the fun things first. Sometimes I put the nasty stuff first to get it out of the way. Sometimes I split an ugly job into fifteen-minute segments with something fun interspersed, like maybe clean two cupboard shelves, have tea, clean out two kitchen drawers, read two chapters of a novel. There's just no end to the creativity involved in this whole process.

I know that there are people who make it through life very successfully without a list. But how could anyone shop for groceries without a list? I tried it once. I was in the middle of making cookies when I realized I was out of flour. I thought, "As long as I have to run to the store for flour, I might as well get a dozen eggs since I used the last one. Certainly I don't need a list for two items."

I got home with my three bags and two boxes of groceries and 120 pounds of softener salt. It was on sale. Oops! No flour and eggs. Back to making lists.

It's impossible to measure the satisfaction that comes from having crossed everything off the list before the sun sets but some things are always number 12 priority and I seldom make it past number 10. Actually, "clean the oven" has been on the list since I baked that apple pie for the Thanksgiving. Why clean it now? I might bake another one for next Sunday's dinner.

Once I was lamenting to my friend that I hadn't finished everything on my list. She said simply, "You have too much on your list!"

Easy for her to say. She doesn't do lists.

I make lists of lists because I keep losing my lists. A couple of months ago while cleaning out the walk-in closet (on the list for a year and a half) I found a size twelve shirt that I had cut out to sew for my son. He now wears a man's size small. Apparently that project was on a list I lost.

I started a list of New Year's resolutions. My first resolution was "quit making lists." But then I thought, "I can't do that. It seems to me that a listless life would be a hopeless life."

I crossed off my first resolution.

Where there's a list, there's hope.

When Too Much Is Not Enough

In a silly song from years ago, a kernel of popcorn is singing, "It's hot on the bottom, want to get up on top. But it seems like I'm just too pooped to pop."

A phrase from a more recent song says, "Too much is not enough."

That doesn't make sense. Or does it?

Exhaustion. Battle fatigue. Nervous breakdown. Stress. Burnout. The terminology changes from year to year. No matter how we describe it, many Americans are just plain tired.

We have more things and enjoy ourselves and others less. We have adequate food for our needs but we want more and even after a meal of over-indulgence, we look for something more to munch on. We have an adequate wardrobe, but we want the latest styles, the brand names. Even after the closet is bulging, we want more. We want bigger houses, newer cars, more money in the bank.

Too much is not enough.

Families are pulled in many directions. If both parents work or operate a business, they may feel guilty for not spending enough time with their children. If the mother works in the home, she may feel guilty for not doing enough, or perhaps other people expect her to volunteer more than she wants to because, after all, she doesn't work. Demands of community, church, and school can become so heavy that no time is left for family. Parents and children feel confused and burned out.

Too much is not enough.

Most single-parent families would prefer not to be. The parent, man or woman, single for whatever reason, struggles to provide a normal family life. He or she has to cover all bases, financial planning, emotional needs, spiritual values, education, work, transportation, home maintenance and repair, cooking, and laundry, and still squeeze in time for church, school, and community activities. Sometimes there isn't enough energy for one person to do it all.

Too much is not enough.

A high school student may be driven either by her own high expectations of herself or in order to fulfill expectations of others. Parents sometimes demand perfection and expect her to be a winner. She has to have all A's. She has to be in all three sports programs. She has to be involved in, and be the best in, band, chorus, drama, church youth group. No matter how much she does, she feels like she should be doing more. She may become irritable, depressed, or physically ill.

Too much is not enough.

A farmer works 18 hours a day during planting and harvesting seasons. He has to work hard so he can support his family and pay for the land, the machinery, the hired help. When everything is paid for, and sometimes before, he needs more land and more machinery. If the crops are poor, he gets more and more behind. No matter how hard he works, he can't seem to get it all done and he can't seem to pay all the bills. He grows weary and there's no time for his wife and children. There's no time to visit with the neighbors like he used to before too much was not enough.

The demands don't necessarily end in retirement. The concept that doing is more important than being dies hard. The retiree may believe that a day spent relaxing, reading, or visiting with friends is wasted. He has grown up with the belief that self-worth depends upon accomplishment. He thinks, "I haven't accomplished anything today, therefore, I am useless."

So he keeps going, doing, joining, running, and volunteering until he wears himself out.

Too much is not enough.

Can we get off the merry-go-round before we burn out or break down? Can we simplify our lives to allow enough time for rest, relaxation, and just plain fun without feeling guilty?

What do we do when too much is not enough?

Soothing Sounds

Sometimes I can hear God speaking, not in an audible voice, but through sounds that give me comfort and a sense of peace or a certain sound can bring to mind a scene from my past which made me feel secure and loved.

Memories take me back to the sound of Dad shaking the ashes down in the wood-burning stove in the living room before he went to bed. I burrowed into the thick feather bed knowing that I would be warm and safe through the cold winter night. In the morning, my alarm clock was the clinking of the metal spoon against the side of the large brown mixing bowl as Mother beat the batter for our daily breakfast pancakes.

Visiting friends and relatives was our major source of entertainment. Crinkling noises in the kitchen meant that we would be offered peppermints, or better yet, chocolate. We kids tried to stay awake long enough in the evening to have coffee and a Spam sandwich with the grown-ups, but we nearly always fell asleep to the drone of voices and the shuffling of cards. When we heard bursts of laughter, we knew someone had surprised their opponents with a trump card or related a hilarious grown-up story.

When I hear a haunting, lonesome train whistle I remember the time my young son and I rode a train for 26 hours when we traveled from Spokane to Jamestown. We both fell asleep to the hypnotic rhythm of the wheels on the track.

If I wake up an hour before I need to get up, I can linger in bed and listen to the plaintive cooing of the mourning doves.

When my brother takes his family camping he chooses a spot beside a river or a waterfall, any place that has the sound of a "babbling brook."

I enjoy spending time in a cabin beside a lake with sounds of water lapping the shore as the sunset is reflected on the rolling waves.

On a dreary day I snuggle under a flannel-backed quilt to read a good book while the raindrops fall gently on the roof and a log crackles in the fireplace.

Whether popcorn is popped in a skillet on the stove, made in an air-popper, or a bag in a microwave it means family and friends sitting in the living room on a Sunday night.

In the backyard, the leaves of the poplar trees whisper summer secrets in the gentle breeze while the frogs croak and splash in the nearby water and the chickadees stake out their favorite territory at the bird feeder.

People who grow up in the city no doubt find comfort in the familiarity of traffic noises and lots-of-people noises, but silence speaks eloquently to the spirits of country people.

Only in Ellendale

I have spent most of my adult life in Ellendale, North Dakota, a small town with a population of under 2,000. If you live in any small town in the upper Midwest, I'll bet you can insert the name of your town wherever Ellendale appears. Some of the things that happen in my town seem out-of-the-ordinary to people accustomed to big-city life. To the "natives," these happenings are simply ordinary.

A farmer near Ellendale left his truck in his field while he plowed. When he came back to his truck, he discovered that a small toolbox and his brown-bag lunch had been stolen. This story made the front page of the local paper.

Only in Ellendale.

Everybody waves at everybody else. If I don't recognize the person I meet, I lift an index finger off the steering wheel just in case I should know him, or he will think he's being ignored. A definite recognition calls for a whole-hand lift from the steering wheel. If I meet a very close friend, he receives a prolonged wave and a cheesy grin.

I always wave at the good ol' boys in the black hats. They always wave at me and there's no telling what they might do if I don't wave back.

Only in Ellendale.

People call me by my mother's first name because I remind them of her.

Only in Ellendale.

If Grandpa is backing out of a parking space, everybody graciously stops and waits for him. Then they wait some more while he signals left, then signals right, then goes straight ahead at six miles-per-hour with his foot on the brake. Nobody honks a horn or yells obscenities.

Only in Ellendale.

It is impossible to be a jogger. I tried it twice. The first time I was offered a ride by five people within six blocks. It really slowed me down. After all, I knew all five of them and we had to talk for awhile. The second time I tried jogging, I was nearly run over by the entire high school track team out for practice on Cemetery Road. I gave up. It just wasn't worth the risk.

Only in Ellendale.

I went into the hardware store to get a can of sheetrock filler for patching a hole in the wall. After making a dollar-fifty purchase, I got a half-hour lesson on how to repair the hole in the wall.

Only in Ellendale.

I missed church two Sundays in a row. My Dad and three other people called me to see if I was sick, and someone put me on the prayer chain.

Only in Ellendale.

Everyone knows everyone else's children. If a child has done some mischief, someone in the community will assume the responsibility of scolding the child soundly, and calling the mother to tell her what should be done to remedy the situation.

Only in Ellendale.

I went into the local cafe to have lunch with Maria. I didn't see Maria, but on the front table were Maria's books, shopping bags, and open purse. So I sat down and waited for her.

Only in Ellendale.

I overheard two Trinity Bible College students talking. One of them said, "John called and asked me how to get to the campus from Highway

281. I told him, 'Just go north until you come to the stop light, hang a right, and go as far as you can go.' John said, 'Which stop light?' and I said, 'Not to worry! There's only one.'"

Only in Ellendale.

People give directions according to where things used to be. "Turn left by the old Johnson house and go south where the cream station used to be." The locals understand that.

Only in Ellendale.

Someone called me and got a wrong number. I recognized the voice and told him the number of the person he was trying to call.

Only in Ellendale.

Last fall during hunting season a couple of out-of-state hunters made arrangements to meet the county auditor on Saturday morning at the courthouse to buy their licenses. My friend, Deb, was running her Saturday morning errands and saw the auditor in the clothing store. He mentioned to Deb that his hunters hadn't shown up at the courthouse yet and he'd have to go back up there and wait for them. Deb went into the craft store to do some shopping and when she came out, she saw a couple of strangers in an out-of-state truck. She walked up to them and said, "I'll bet you're looking for the auditor. He's across the street in the clothing store."

Only in Ellendale.

Recently I was having a bad day, and I was beginning to think that there is no joy, peace, kindness, love, justice, or mercy left in the world. Then my neighbor plowed my garden and wouldn't take any pay, my friend invited me out for coffee, a customer thanked me for a job well done, and someone I didn't recognize said, "Hello." A spark of hope leaped up inside me and a wave of thankfulness for small-town living swept over me as I took inventory of the many blessings God has given me.

Only in Ellendale.

*Country-fied
isn't like it
used to be*

Transitions

I'm a girl of the Dakota prairies – transplanted to a small Dakota town. My daughter is a small-town girl – transplanted to the city of Denver. My roots pull me back to the golden wheat fields and the grassy pastures where I ran barefoot with carefree abandon. I try to be contented with my life in a small town with a small-town job, small-town politics, small-town friendliness, and small-town gossip.

And yet, my creative spirit longs for the "something more" in the lifestyle which my citified daughter has chosen.

My parents were married during the Depression. Their lives and philosophy were deeply affected by those times. I can still hear them say things like, "You want new shoes? What's wrong with the old pair?"

"If you can't pay cash for it, you don't need it."

"Hang on to the money you have. You may not get any more."

My daughter might say, "You want new shoes? Buy six pairs, you deserve them. Buy now, build up your credit. What's money for but to enjoy? There's more where this came from."

I'm somewhere between those two philosophies. I don't want to feel guilty about buying a pair of shoes before the old pair is beyond hope, but on the other hand I don't want to have the guilt of spending too much on myself. I want to save, but I also want to enjoy what I've earned.

There were topics and feelings which were simply understood to be taboo when I was a child. We didn't discuss sex, why Grandpa got a divorce years ago, or how angry we were at Dad. Ladies whom we knew *never* swore.

For my daughter, no topic is off-limits, no feelings withheld from discussion. The attitude is that it's healthy to open up and express your feelings. Let it all hang out.

There are topics and feelings which I wish I could have discussed and expressed with my parents, and yet there are things I don't want my daughter to tell me. I often mask my true feelings and try to show the world that I'm in control and yet there are times when I take off the mask and dance for joy in my kitchen with my young son.

I long for the slower pace of country life – to be able to watch a butterfly while I hoe the carrots or to enjoy a silence so deep that the only

147

sound is the song of the meadow lark.

I wonder if I could ever adapt to city ways – traffic, noise, traffic, larger schools, traffic, larger shopping malls, traffic.

I am no longer "just a housewife" as my mother was, nor am I a corporate executive. I'm caught somewhere in between with what my parents call a career and my daughter calls a dead-end job.

.....and Prairie Wind beckons, "Come back to me. You will never be free from my hold on you. Your roots are too deep. You belong to me."

.....and Big City entices, "Come. Find excitement and fulfillment and opportunity beyond your wildest dreams. Come."

.....but Small Town cautions, "Stay where you are. Don't take chances. You might get hurt. You might fail. You might forget where you came from. Don't go."

As I struggle with my identity and with where I belong, I am reminded that wherever I choose to live, whatever my career choice, God has promised to be with me. He was with my parents as they farmed the land and He will be with my children wherever the circumstances of life take them. Times change, people change, but God remains the same forever.

When I Learn to Play the Game of Life Somebody Changes the Rules

Whenever I begin to feel comfortable with things the way they are, I discover that they no longer are that way. The one constant in life seems to be change and sometimes I wish things could stay the same.

The rules of our society in general seem to have changed. It seems that the minority rules. The majority is silent. The criminal gets the justice. Final adoptions are no longer final. Christianity is termed the "counter-culture." Invasion of privacy is a common occurrence. These changes are cause for concern.

Change is evident in specific matters of everyday life. The doctor or dentist was always old enough to be my father. Now the doctor or dentist is old enough to be my son or daughter. It's not easy to take advice seriously from someone who looks young enough to be a college freshman.

If a man asks the token woman in an office to pour him a cup of coffee, she's likely to ask him if his arm is broken. If a man opens a door for a lady, she may let him know that she is perfectly capable of opening her own doors. It's a no-win situation.

Farmers no longer use the manila-colored *Farm Account Record Book*. They put their cows and bushels of barley on database.

The new rule seems to be, "Why keep it simple if it can be made difficult?" Take this example of what you have to go through to get a telephone hooked up. It used to be a simple matter. You just called the local telephone man (who is now called Communications Technician) and in less than 30 minutes the phone was in and ringing. Now you must dial a series of numbers, each of which is answered by a recording with further instructions. Eventually, you may be fortunate enough to reach a real live person, who probably has a Boston accent. He takes your request for a phone installation. He calls the Communications Technician with whom you had morning coffee an hour ago and presto! Four days later your phone is in and ringing.

My record albums are warping on the shelf. I can't find a turn table for playing them. I used a cassette player for tapes until my daughter got a boom box. When my son said, "I'm buying some CD's," I said, "Good for you! You're finally saving some money. I'm proud of you."

He looked at me like I had just grown two heads and explained that a CD is a compact disc and costs twice as much as a tape. So much for frugality.

We used to go out to watch a movie. Stores were all closed on Sundays so we either stayed home or visited neighbors. Since there was no TV, we made up games and activities without spending money. Lest I become too nostalgic, I must ask myself whether or not I would really like to go back to the good old days, the days of outhouses and no electricity, no air-conditioning and no hot, running water.

In spite of cries of the complexity of technology there are certain inventions I'd hate to live without. My life has been made wonderfully simpler with the microwave, the computer, and the copy machine. And believe it or not, I was able to learn how to use these machines after the old age of 40!

Yes, I realize that the only constant in life, aside from God, is change. I can either go with the flow or drown in a sea of inaccurate memories of how things used to be. I hope that, as long as I live, I will look forward to the next challenge of learning something new without forgetting the solid values of my heritage.

Coffee Choices

I stepped up to the counter in Ye Olde Coffee Shoppe and said to the young waiter with a pony tail and an earring in his eyebrow, "Coffee, please."

"What flavor, Ma'am?"

"Coffee with cream, please."

He gave me a condescending look. "We don't have that. The choices are listed on the board."

"Oh," I said, feeling somewhat ignorant regarding the latest trends in coffee.

I offered my place in line to the sweet young blonde in the black leather mini-skirt and hiking boots while I studied the 10'x10' board behind the counter.

My coffee vocabulary consists of Folgers, Butternut, black, with cream or sugar. There were words and concepts on that menu I'd never heard before.

Light roast, traditional roast, Stockholm roast, dark roast, Espresso, Columbia, Costa Rica pea berry, mocha java, Kenya, Kona, Alto Grande, cappuccino, latte.

I had no idea what a latte was, but it sounded sophisticated, so I said, "A large latte, please."

Again, the waiter said, "What flavor, Ma'am?"

"Oh. I have to make another choice. Let me look over the options again."

I stepped aside to let him wait on the man in the impeccable business suit. Of course, he knew exactly what he wanted.

"Chocolate raspberry cappuccino, please," he said.

"That sounds disgusting," I thought as I pored over the flavors list.

Hazelnut, turtle pecan, mocha, cinnamon, amaretto, caramel, tooti-fruiti, butter rum, butterscotch, macadamia, peppermint stick, Irish creme, French vanilla, Swiss chocolate. The note at the bottom of the menu said, "You may choose one flavor or any combination of flavors."

I thought, "My goodness! Am I in a coffee house or candy store?"

"Sir, I've decided on a large butter rum latte!"

He looked relieved as he pushed the ON button and the machine started making noises like a combine in a Dakota wheat field. He said,

"Would you like whipped cream on top?"

"Is that real cream or are you using non-fat dairy substitute?" I asked.

He was beginning to get testy. He said, "Take your pick, lady!"

One more decision was too much for me. I said, "Why don't you just give me a cup of hot tea?"

He threw the latte in the sink and said, "Will that be orange pekoe, green, oolong, black, Earl Grey, English breakfast, Ceylon cinnamon, jasmine whisper, honey ginseng mint, lemon berry breeze, chamomile dream, strawberry spice, apple zinger.............

Clotheslines

Clotheslines told stories. In the beginning the family's clothes on the line consisted of "his" and "hers." Soon crib sheets and diapers flapped in the wind beside the overalls and house dresses. The passage of time was marked with rompers, pinafores, school dresses and jeans, confirmation dresses, and wedding shirts. Sometimes Grandpa and Grandma clothes appeared as families cared for the elderly in their homes.

Then one day Mother and Dad looked at the clothesline where once again only "his" and "hers" were drying. "Where have the years gone?" they asked.

Monday was always wash day, unless, of course it was pouring rain. If there were just a few sprinkles, "it might clear off," so we took a chance.

Dad always carried the buckets of water from the cistern and emptied them into the copper boiler on the kerosene stove in the kitchen. Then the pails of hot water were carried to the wash house and dumped into the tub of the wringer washing machine. We sliced Fels Naptha into the boiling water and put bluing into the rinse water. The gasoline motor had to be started like a motorcycle and made as much noise. While the first load of clothes was washing, the Argo starch was boiled and prepared for shirts, blouses, skirts, and dresses.

As soon as a child was tall enough to reach a clothesline, Mother had "help." Hanging out the wash was my favorite job. I always hung towels together, pants together, socks in a row, bloomers from little to big. We could hang out our unmentionables as we knew nobody was going to come on Monday. All the neighbors were home hanging out their own unmentionables. Mother hung her basketful of clothes in any order as they came out of the basket. It was quicker that way, she said, but I wanted everything organized.

I took my time, to feel the coolness of the wet clothes on a hot summer day. When it was colder outside, I sorted the clothes in the wash house so it would be quicker, but they were still "in order."

The clothes were hung outside, even in freezing weather. When the frozen clothes were carried into the house the four of us children would dance with Dad's frozen underwear before we hung them on clotheslines strung up from one door frame to another where they finished drying over night. The clothes made eerie silhouettes and scary shadows on the wall at night. I could imagine badgers with bared teeth and long claws or coyotes crouching, ready to pounce.

In the summertime we made blanket tents over the clotheslines. Our imaginations ran wild as we made secret passages and put rocks, boards, and bricks around the edges of the blankets to anchor them and to keep the skunks and rattlesnakes out. Once or twice we got brave enough to sleep in our tent overnight – very little sleep with all those worries about skunks, rattlesnakes, and coyotes.

After I was married and living in a small town I still hung my clothes on the line. I loved the fresh-air smell of line-dried clothes. I chose a lovely day, not necessarily Monday, so I could take my time. I leisurely pinned up the clothes while I looked at my flower beds, watched the neighbor's children at play, and wiggled my bare toes in the cool green lawn grass. My own baby cooed on her blanket in the shade of the cottonwood tree. She played with her toes, reached for blades of grass, and laughed at the clothes fluttering above her in the wind.

I continued to hang clothes out whenever I could even when I had a full-time job. Sometimes I'd hang them out after work and leave them on the line overnight, something my mother would never have done.

Times change, we progress. I use a washer and dryer. The fresh-air scent is provided by scented dryer sheets. I don't have to pay attention to rain, wind, snow, or sunshine and I appreciate the convenience.

But on a Monday when the air smells fresh, the sun is high in the sky, and a gentle south wind caresses me, I miss my clothesline.

Gender Bias

My parents were ahead of their time. They believed that their kids could do everything and be anything they wanted to be and they paid little attention to gender stereotypes.

They set their hands to the tasks that needed to be done. Mother was a better carpenter than Dad was. She built the bookcase from an old pump organ, she built storage chests and fixed the cupboard doors. When she was young, she broke horses to the saddle. Dad washed dishes and carried wash water on laundry days. I especially remember the corn fritters he had ready for us to eat when Mother had spent a long day of shopping with the four of us. They believed that both men and women should take leadership roles in the church and in the community.

I spent a lot of time as a small child following Dad around outside. I watched as he repaired tractor engines. He took the outsides off and I could see how the insides worked. I was fascinated by wheels and cogs turning and odd-looking pieces moving up and down.

I played with my brother's tinker toys and Lincoln logs more than he did and I never liked playing house or dolls or dressing up in fancy play clothes like my girlfriend did. I felt better in faded blue jeans, climbing on haystacks or swinging from a trapeze slung from the barn rafters. And I put my own angleworms on my fishhooks, thank you.

In our country school everybody did handcrafts during the cold winter recesses. The girls did woodworking and the boys learned embroidery or vice versa as the spirit moved. We didn't pay attention to boys' projects or girls' projects, we just did whatever appealed to us.

I could write my numbers at age four and during the first week that I was in school the teacher gave me a little yellow math workbook. I said, "How much should I do?"

She said, "Just work as far as you can and I'll help you if you need me." It was so simple. When she came back to check on me I was on page 27 and she couldn't believe it.

But somewhere along the line I got the message that boys are supposed to be better at math than girls are, and that motors are boys' stuff. My parents didn't teach me that. Society did. I started to avoid math in school if I had a choice. I quit looking at motors and started saying things like, "I don't have a mechanical mind. I'm not good at math," and soon I had convinced myself that I was, indeed, not good at those things.

I became more aware of the types of behavior society expected of men and women. As a teenager I got upset with girls who played the "oh-dear-poor-little-weak-ol'-me" game in order to get the boys to notice them. And I was always amazed at how the boys fell all over themselves to come to their rescue. It was disgusting, perhaps only because it never worked for me. I could usually figure out how to do things myself and I couldn't pretend that I didn't know how to do something when I did know how just to get attention.

Stereotypes die hard, if at all. When I'm the only woman on a committee and someone needs to be the secretary, guess who gets appointed. If someone hands me the pen I hand it back and say, "Sorry. I'm a creative writer and I never stick to the facts. Better give it to someone else."

If someone walks into a business looking for the owner or the president, the assumption is that a man is in charge.

Men are proud of a son who is the quarterback on the football team or top scorer on the basketball floor. I know of a young man who wanted to be a chef. His father was not impressed and sent him to college to become an accountant because he was good at math like boys are supposed to be.

He was an obedient son and he got his accounting degree to please his father. He is now happily working as a chef.

A lot of men have the idea that they have to have sons in order to prove their manhood. My mother always said, "So what's wrong with having girls?"

I was impressed with something Garth Brooks said in an interview. His wife had just given birth to their second daughter. Someone in the audience asked him if he was going to try for a boy the third time. He said, "If we have another one, it would be just fine if we had another girl. I like my girls."

I thought, "Good for you, Garth Brooks," and I went out and bought his latest tape.

I always admired the Eleanor Roosevelts and the Marie Curies in the world. They are examples of strong women with missions. It takes courage for women to be strong because a lot of men don't like strong women and a lot of women don't like strong women. It takes a strong man to love and appreciate a strong woman.

Most women don't want to better themselves by putting men down. That is not true equality. I hope that my children will see a day when the person qualified for or suited to a job is the person chosen for that job. I hope that men and women will quit playing bash-the-opposite-sex games and truly learn to respect one another.

J Want My Rights

Article I of the Bill of Rights: "Congress shall make no law respecting an establisment of religion, or prohibiting the free exercise thereof; or abridging the freedom of speech, or of the press; or the right of the people peaceably to assemble, and to petition the government for a redress of grievances."

That's it. Short and to the point.

I wonder if our forefathers might be turning over in their graves if they could see what is being done in the name of First Amendment rights. I'm sure they would be amazed at the volumes upon volumes which have been written to try to interpret and judge Article I.

People are screaming that they have the right to print, to write, to paint, to speak anything they darn well please and nobody better interfere with their "rights."

We have 6,000,000,000 people in the world and theoretically they can all be screaming for "my rights." We want all 6,000,000,000 people to have their rights. After all, democracy is based on the premise of the rights of individuals. Too many countries do not have the wonderful freedom that we in America take for granted.

Does this "right" include the right of painting and displaying sacrilegious pictures – for example – the Virgin Mary plastered with elephant dung? Does it include reporting every facet and detail of a president's affair with his intern? Does it include prying into the lives of private citizens?

Yes, I suppose an artist has the right to paint and sell irreverent garbage, but I also have the right to refuse to display it, to look at it, to acknowledge it as "art." A reporter has the right to investigate the affairs of public officials, but where do they cross the line of respect for privacy?

When I hear of dispicable things being done in the name of First Amendment rights, I can't help but wonder. Have we no fear of God, no respect for the holy and the sacred? Have we completely lost our sense of decency? Have we no sense of beauty and refinement? Have we no aspirations to creativity which produces writing and art and music which uplift the spirit, enlighten the soul?

Perhaps if nobody paid any attention to disrepectful "artworks" and ignored the misguided people who are crying for attention in this negative way, they would just go away, but I don't think so. When culture starts to spiral downward, it takes great effort to spiral it upward.

When television shows and movies started to allow the use of one or two four-letter words, people were shocked. They said, "How could they do that? Isn't that against FCC guidelines?" but others said, "According to the First Amendment, we have the right to say anything we want to say."

So the downward spiral continues to spiral downward as four-letter words become so common that we hardly notice and the shock value is reduced to tolerance and tolerance is reduced to, "It's my right to say anything I want to say."

What would happen if the media refused to publicize and in a negative sense glorify the shootings and bomb threats in the nation's schools? Wouldn't it be more effective to leave the incidents up to the individual communities without the focus of national coverage? Doesn't this over-coverage give more students the ideas and the information they need to commit similar crimes?

What have we heard lately about the "R" word, the word "responsibility?"

Yes, the media has the right to cover these events, but what about the media's responsibility not to sensationalize? How much knowledge does the public really need?

When I was growing up without the blessing of television, the only violence I saw was Mother killing a chicken for Sunday dinner. Now we see violence on the television screen so often that we no longer feel anything when we see it. We are desensitized. As adults we know that much of what we see is not real, but our very young children cannot discern reality from unreality.

How often I hear, "It's up to a parent to monitor the programs their children watch."

It should be so simple.

Even as we watch good programs, we are forced to endure graphic and unacceptable commercials for upcoming programs which pop up unexpectedly during breaks. Our children go to visit friends whose parents don't do the monitoring they should be doing. Parents have to work to put food on the table, so children are home after school for a couple of hours without supervision. They watch anything and everything. I'm not too worried about parents who monitor their children's television viewing and discuss programs with them, but what about those children who lack that type of supervision?

Doesn't society have a responsibility for protecting all children? Doesn't anybody care?

Think of raising children. When they are young, every decision is made for them because they don't have the ability to make their own decisions wisely or the sense of responsibility for accepting the consequences of their decisions. When they reach high school age, they stamp their feet and cry for their independence, "When I leave home and am on my own, I'll be able to do anything I want to do."

Parents smile, because they know that when children leave home, they may do anything they please for a while, but will soon realize that they have the enormous responsibility of making wise decisions, decisions that will be good not only for them and their own families, but also good for the community and society in general.

They will need to choose the actions and lifestyles that will please God.

A nation that screams for rights without responsibilities cannot long endure.

Labor-Saving Technology

There was a time when farmers worked from the time the sun came up in the morning until the sun went down in the evening. The work may have been physically hard during the day, but when the sun went down, there was little that could be done without daylight. People gathered around the kerosene lamp to read or perhaps write a letter and they rested a lot.

Then came the miracle. Electricity!

Life is good. No more heating sad irons on a kerosene stove, just plug the iron into the socket. No more running outside to the cellar to get cool milk and butter, just open the refrigerator. We can see well enough to wash dishes and scrub floors until midnight.

With electricity in their shops, farmers are able to work on their machinery after dark. Since tractors have headlights and heated cabs, farmers can work in their fields all night if they so choose. Fifty years ago, who would have believed that farmers would be given the opportunity of combining in December in the Dakotas?

With bigger farm tractors and more machinery, a farmer needs more land to justify the purchase of the expensive equipment and when he gets more land, he needs bigger seeders to cover the ground more quickly so he has more time to cover more ground. And if the farmers don't already have enough to do, or the price they get for grain and livestock isn't enough to cover the cost of their farming operation and support a family, they can get jobs in a factory which operates with shifts around the clock.

Most women in the Dakotas, including farm women, work outside the home, so we need more clothes. Caring for the clothing is easier than it was in Grandma's day when she devoted all day Monday to washing and all day Tuesday to ironing. We can just toss the clothes into the washer while we clean or cook or spend a few precious minutes with children after eight hours of working for pay.

Everywhere we look, we see new gadgets and inventions. Some of them are wonderful and we wonder how we ever got along without them. Take the world of quilting for example. Great-grandma cut each piece individually from scraps she had available and stitched the blocks together by hand. She was proud of herself when she finished one quilt during the long winter. She would be astonished to visit a quilt shop today and find rotary cutters, self-healing cutting mats, hard plastic rulers and templates that don't bend and get out of shape with repeated tracing and cutting. These inventions are so wonderful that we can now whack a three-yard cut of fabric into strips and blocks in less than an hour and make a quilt in a day instead of one per winter. Then we can buy more $8- per-yard cotton to make more quilts to use up more of the time we saved.

With the computer explosion we should in theory become a paperless society. We can get on the Internet to do our research and send our letters by e-mail. We should be able to save a few trees if not an entire forest.

Quite the opposite has happened. BC (Before Computers) secretaries typed individual letters to clients and customers. Now businesses print out tons of brochures and personalized letters by using the marvelous print-merge and the search-and-replace features on computers. The letters sound like the company president is talking to us personally. Isn't it wonderful that now we can get ten previously approved credit card applications in our mail each week instead of one or two a year which we might receive had they been typed? Oh, well. The use of all that paper gives the mail carriers and the lumberjacks job security and gives EPA a purpose for existing.

We now have thousands of choices for jobs and activities. Many of us have difficulty in limiting our choices and try to do it all. We do more work so we can make more money and have more things, oftentimes at the expense of relationships with family or friends. Instead of using technology wisely to make our lives simpler, we are being driven by it and letting it control us.

In a nation with such an abundance of material goods and such a myriad of choices, we are encouraged to believe in the illusion that if we work hard enough and long enough, we can have anything and everything we want. The stark reality for most of us is that we can't have it all, do it all, be it all.

We have been like the proverbial dog chasing its tail. He runs fast but doesn't accomplish anything that really matters.

The Godstick

Homer and Sadie, lovable, gentle, quiet people, become control freaks when they get the remote control in their hands. They jokingly call the remote the Godstick because whoever has it is in charge. It's a phenomenon neither one of them can explain.

Homer, in typically male fashion, watches four shows at one time which drives Sadie crazy.

"Click, click, click."

The remote lets him get in on snippets of "Frasier," "Home Improvement," "Larry King Live," and "Prime Time Country" all in the same time slot.

He hasn't seen a commercial in six months. Whenever a commercial comes on, it's surf time. He thinks he's outsmarting the advertisers, but Sadie is quick to point out that advertisers have outsmarted him by using the product placement style of advertising. She notes that while he surfs, he's sipping the same soft drink that his favorite actor is drinking on the sitcom.

When Sadie wanted to eat popcorn and watch "The Bridges of Madison County" without interruption, she hid the Godstick in the clothes hamper. She conveniently forgot where she hid it, so she had four days of watching shows from beginning to end until Homer did laundry and happened to find it.

Then there was the time when Homer programmed the VCR to record their favorite shows while they were gone for the week-end. When they came home and sat down to watch their programs, no one could find the remote. A week later, one of the kids found it in the puppy's house.

Sadie likes her quilting, cooking, and home decorating shows. She was not a happy camper when Homer flicked the Godstick to watch "NASCAR" while she was watching "Chef Marian" and she missed the list of ingredients for the cream sauce for asparagus.

She got even with him. While he was watching the Twins game, she clicked over to "Interior Motives" and he missed the winning home run and didn't know the score until he watched the evening news.

Sadie doesn't believe the statisticians when they say the main causes of divorce in America are lack of communication, abuse, infidelity, or money matters.

She knows that the first question a marriage counselor asks a couple on the brink of disaster is, "Do you have a remote control?"

If the answer is yes, the second question is, "Who controls the remote control and why?"

Going Global

Sometimes I don't listen to the news for two or three weeks at a time. It becomes more than I can bear to listen to another story of horror and tragedy. I am overwhelmed with reports of a crisis in every nation, with wars and atrocities and persecutions, with graphic depictions of starvation and human suffering in inhuman conditions. I can't listen to one more problem which I can't solve or one more desperate need which I can't fulfill.

The stories have always been there, but now they are brought into our living rooms on a daily basis through the magic of multi-media technology.

The concept of neighbor is being redefined. The global society is telling me that everyone is my neighbor. Everyone is my responsibility. I feel helpless, insignificant, and lost. I'd like to go away somewhere to escape from all of the responsibilities that are being put in my path.

But there is no escape.

How do we handle the pace at which everything is moving? How do we get along with people on the other side of the earth when we can't get along with our own family members or neighbors?

How do we deal with a global economy? Do we understand global economics? I certainly don't, but I don't have to be a rocket scientist to figure out that the global economy is affecting me.

Banks are merging into larger and ever-larger entities.

The mortgage that I obtained locally has been sold out-of-state three times.

When I had a question about my surgery bill, I talked to somebody in Ohio. I threw away the first statement they sent me because I don't know anyone in Ohio and I thought it was another piece of junk mail offering me a credit card at a rate too good to pass up. Perhaps next month someone in France will do the surgeon's collecting, who knows?

If I want to make a quilt, I find that cotton fabric can now cost me seven or eight dollars a yard. I need at least five yards for the back and six yards for piecing the top. Even if I'm fortunate enough to get it for $4 a yard, the fabric will cost me $44. The batting will be a minimum of $7, more if I want top quality. Add in the price of the thread at $4 and I've already invested $55 excluding labor.

I pick up a copy of a Sunday paper and find a circular which advertises hand-made comforters, any size for $39. Guess how they do that!

I sell a doily for $10 and consider that a bargain until I see one of the same size and equal quality for $2 in a craft shop. I wonder how much the poor Oriental lady (or child) gets for working a whole day on it.

American companies are setting up their factories and businesses where they can get the cheapest labor. How about a dollar an hour in Mexico and a quarter an hour in China?

Yes, all people are entitled to a job. Yes, even poor Americans are rich by global standards. Are we ready to sacrifice our own jobs or receive lower wages so people in other nations can have a decent standard of living? Will I have to lower my standard of living so that others may live?

Who is my neighbor?

These are hard questions and they are not going to go away.

$\mathcal{P}lug$ $\mathcal{I}n$ or $\mathcal{T}une$ $Out?$

We go to our mailboxes each day in anticipation of something good, a letter from a friend, the book we ordered two weeks ago, the weekly newspaper, or a check from Publisher's Clearing House. What we are more apt to get is a handful of pre-approved applications for credit cards or a survey to fill out in return for coupons or free samples.

Something free sounds like a plan so we decide to fill out the survey. We start answering questions and checking the boxes in front of the products we use. We do all right with the first few questions. Which cereal does your family eat most often? What brand of laundry soap do you use? How many miles per day do people in your household drive to work? Then we come to the more personal questions. What are the ages of the members of your household? How many packs of cigarettes does the head of the household smoke per week? Does the head of the household wear dentures? Is the head of the household currently on a diet or taking anti-depressant medications?

Wait a minute! Who wants to know? And why do they want to know? We begin to realize that people 1500 miles away are going to know more about us than our own children know. We start to wonder what those people are going to do with all of this wonderful knowledge that we have so generously provided them in exchange for a few cents off on a box of Wheat Yummies. If this information is fed into computers, which we assume it will be, who will have access to this information and why?

Does this concept scare us? Should it scare us?

Things are changing so rapidly. Whether we live in the city or in the country is immaterial, we are affected by these changes.

Imagine for a moment the concept of your television set being connected with a computer, telephone, fax machine, and copy machine. Also wired into this system is your bank account and bill paying system.

Let your mind wander and you can add numerous other possibilities for technological enhancements. (No article about computers is complete without a form of the word enhance.) Picture also that these systems are as common in our homes a few years from now as the telephone and television are today. Since we already have those, why not just plug in a few more machines?

It becomes mind-boggling to think of the possibilities for using such systems. We all know about e-mail and surfing the World Wide Web. But imagine advertisers customizing their ads through our television sets. We could receive only the ads targeted to our own specific needs and wants. And where will the advertisers get the data for this process? Remember that little survey we filled out for the free samples?

What about the information trail we leave whenever we use a credit card? Each item purchased is scanned and printed on the receipt. Right? We might be surprised at the amount of information that is available to anyone who is actively seeking it.

We are told that we can retain our privacy with the use of encryption on our computers. Think about that one. If someone is smart enough to figure out how to encrypt certainly someone else is smart enough to figure out how to "unencrypt."

We can decide to avoid all this technology by buying a little cabin far, far away in the deep dark forest where there is no electricity or telephone. But even if we do that we will not be able to escape. The computer-generated, tailor-made junk mail will somehow find its way to our secluded mailbox offering us quality bearskin rug-making services and uncarded wool for our spinning wheels.

When Driving Drives Me Crazy

When I was a teenager, I loved to drive. Couldn't get enough of it. Not any more.

These days, I get into my car with fear and trepidation and offer up a prayer for any available, unemployed angel to act as my shield and protector.

I've had 18-wheelers pass me in no-passing zones in fog as thick as pea soup. Last week I was car number three in a four-car caravan when a truck pulling a long trailer passed all of us. If I were Norwegian, I might have said, "Uff duh!"

Whenever I have a tailgater I swear I'm going to patent this neat little invention. Whenever the magic eye determines that a car is 15.5 feet from my rear bumper, the trunk flies open and a huge sign pops up that says, "Beware. I brake for squirrels, bunny rabbits, and kitty cats."

I'm always puzzled about what to do when I'm following someone who is either drunk or talking on a cell phone. He zigzags back and forth from the right-hand side of the white line on the right across the yellow line in the center. Do I pass him and get ahead of him so he can't do something to hurt me or will he hurt me if I try to pass him?

Four-way stops are a quandary. What do I do if we all get there at approximately the same time? If I'm coming from the west in my white Chevy, do I wait for the purple pickup from the south? For whom does the red convertible from the east wait and when does the blue Buick from the north get a chance? Might there be an understanding that certain colors go first? The yield-to-the-right law doesn't seem to apply in this situation. It never fails that there's a gracious gentleman who is frantically waving to everyone else to go ahead. Don't trust him.

When a light turns green and I don't hit the accelerator soon enough I'm guaranteed that there's a cowboy behind me who is late for a rodeo and honks his horn to let me know it. Whenever that happens I have the terrible urge to get out of my car, walk around slowly to look at my tires and pop up my hood to check the windshield washer fluid. This should guarantee that he will have to wait through at least three green lights. If I did this in a small town, he would probably help me with my inspection. Somewhere else I might be beaten with a tire iron.

At least once in a forty-mile trip someone pulls up from a side road and waits and waits and waits, then pulls out in front of me so I have to brake and slow down to 35 mph for two miles.

Diagonal parking on Main Street used to be a simple matter. That was in the days when people drove their cars to town and left their pickups and trucks in the wheat fields or farm yards where they belong. Now I back out of a parking spot at my own risk. I can't see over the sports utility vehicles and I have to back across the street in order to see around the pickup that pulled in after I parked where there were empty spaces on both sides of me.

You'd think people in the Dakotas would know how to take a farmer's corner at an intersection. I stop at a reasonable distance from the stop sign to wait for a car approaching from my right. The driver cuts his left turn so short I can see the color of his eyes.

I'm sure I also do a few things that drive other people crazy. Sometimes I signal left and turn right. Well, that's probably safer than signaling right and turning left. I'm a woman. I can change my mind.

How about those white lines in the shopping mall parking lots? It seems to me they are all painted in the wrong direction. My car won't fit. Oh, well. I can just back into a space and I'll be fine. I usually manage to straddle the white line and take up two spaces. Once I did even better and backed up far enough so I used up four spaces. Pretty good, huh? But strangely, when I drove out I was still going the wrong direction.

Until we live in a perfect world, I'll keep requesting an angel as I buckle up my seat belt and adjust my rear-view mirror. Maybe when you see me coming, you should ask for an angel, too.

"*Your call is very important to us......*"

It happened to me again, but this time I got even.

I had a question which I needed to ask concerning the mortgage on my house.

I had obtained the original mortgage from a local bank to which a phone call would have been no problem at all because a real live person would have answered the phone. However, my mortgage has been sold three times in five years, so when I dialed the 800 number, I had no idea where the telephone person was located.

Dream on, Elaine, if you think a real person is going to pick up the phone.

I was given the three-minute introduction and instructions concerning which button to push if I was calling from a touch-tone phone and advised that if I was using a rotary dial phone, I should stay on the line and I would be connected to an operator.

"If you wish to know your payment status, press 1.

"If you wish to know your loan balance and payoff information, press 2.

"If you wish to know your interest rate, press 3.

"If you wish to refinance your loan, press 4.

"If you wish to apply for a home equity loan, press 5."

Since none of those options addressed the question I wanted to ask, I pretended that I was calling from a rotary dial phone.

I listened politely to the next three minutes of information taped by a woman with an extrememly annoying voice about all of the additional loans and services in which I should certainly be interested.

Then she said, "All operators are currently with our customers. Your call is very important to us. Please hold," and I was serenaded by a bad recording of "Clair de Lune."

After 60 seconds of music, the voice came back on the line with, "Your call is very important to us. Please hold," and another 60 seconds of "Clair de Lune."

After no fewer than ten repetitions of this idiocy, I was just about to hang up when I heard a cheerful, "Good mornin', Ma'am. Thank you for holdin'. How may I he'p you?"

Aha! A real live person at last.

From the accent and the use of the word Ma'am, I could tell she was definitely not from the Dakotas or Minnesota.

I couldn't resist. I said in my sweetest Midwestern dialect, "I'm on another line right now, but my call is very important to your company. Please hold," and I set the receiver down in front of my stereo which was blasting a lively version of Lawrence Welk's "Beer Barrel Polka."

After exactly 60 seconds, I picked up the receiver and said, "Thank you for holding, Ma'am. I am still on another line, but I will be with you momentarily. My call is very important to your company. Please hold."

I set the receiver down in front of Lawrence Welk again and strolled out to the kitchen to pour myself a cup of coffee to drink while I put dinner in the oven.

The Parable of the Peasants

Once upon a time, a long time ago, many peasants owned small tracts of land in the wonderful kingdom of Zenn. They were happy people who worked hard and felt connected to the land they loved. They were proud of their labors which kept the people of Zenn well-fed and warmly clothed by producing grain for bread, and woolen and flaxen fibers for clothing.

But it came to pass in the land of Zenn that the miller decided he wanted more profit for him and his family so he paid the peasants less for their grain and charged the baker more for the bags of flour he milled. Soon he became wealthy. He built a bigger house for himself and his family, and bought expensive clothing and jewels for his wife.

The baker was a bit irritated when the miller charged more for a bag of flour. Since the baker could make many loaves of bread from one bag of flour, he was still making a reasonable profit, but his wife started nagging him.

"Look at the beautiful new house the miller built for his wife. Why can't you build a better one for me? And look at her gorgeous dresses and fine rubies and emeralds. Don't you love me as much as the miller loves his wife?"

The baker truly loved his wife and wanted her to have the best, so he raised the price of each loaf of bread. He thought the townfolks wouldn't notice a small increase and surely they would be willing to pay a little more. What choice did they have if they wanted to eat?

After a few years the peasants realized that they were being paid less and less for their hard work, the miller and the baker were becoming more and more wealthy, and the townfolks were going without bread because they could not afford to pay the increasingly higher costs of a loaf of bread.

Some of the peasants' wives had to get jobs in town in order to buy hoes and sickles for planting and harvesting their crops and to provide educations for their children. Some of the peasants decided they would grow only enough food and raise enough animals for their own use. Some of them decided to store their grain and keep their animals off the market until the prices were high enough for them to make a decent living and a reasonable profit for themselves. The peasants were not happy peasants.

Conditions in the wonderful land of Zenn grew worse as the years passed until the townfolks were going hungry. A large group of them decided to attend the monthly meeting of the Townfolks Council to decide upon a plan of action.

The following week, the members of the Townfolks Council and an entourage of weak but determined men picketed the Royal Castle of the King of Zenn. The townfolks were surprised when the miller and the baker joined the picket line. They, too were hungry as the money and fine jewels they owned could not buy them food that did not exist or was not for sale.

When the King of Zenn realized what was happening, he came out to the picketers and asked to speak with them. The townfolks were amazed that he came out of his castle as he rarely made a public appearance. They were even more amazed by his frail appearance and realized that the King of Zenn was also going hungry.

The King and his subjects had not understood how they were all dependent upon the land from which their food, clothing, and shelters were derived. They expressed a new appreciation and respect for the peasants.

They decided that the peasants deserved an honest price for their labors as well as did the miller and the baker.

When the peasants heard of the picketing, they rejoiced greatly. They opened up their stores of grain then planted enough for all the townfolks for the next year.

After the harvest in the fall, the peasants invited the miller, the baker, the townfolks, the members of the Townfolks Council and the King of Zenn to dance at their Celebration of the Harvest.

And they all lived happily ever after.

If Big Is Good, Is Bigger Better?

Farming isn't like it used to be.

In the good old days almost every section of land supported two families. The tidy farmsteads invariably included white, two-story frame houses. Red barns contained hay mows with stanchions below where a couple of cows were milked twice a day. Chicken coops housed fryers and laying hens. Small herds of contented cattle grazed in green pastures. Grain was stored in the bins for next spring's planting. Cellars held enough potatoes and canned vegetables and fruits to last all winter. Neighbors owned machinery in common or if one owned a combine and another owned a cornpicker, they shared equipment and exchanged work.

Sad to say, it will probably never be like that again.

Large farmers are buying smaller farms to add to their empires.

Large agricultural companies are merging with each other and buying up smaller companies or smaller farms.

Reorganization. Restructuring. Consolidation.

Nice, big words with more than two syllables.

What those big words and intellectual sounding phrases don't say to the employee of a small-town agricultural business when it is closed because of a merger with a larger business is, "You're fired. The job you've done for years no longer exists."

168

The big words don't tell farmers who have been able to drive twenty miles for machinery parts that they now will have to drive eighty miles.

The big words don't mention the loss of families in a small, struggling community where houses sell at a price far below their actual value and other jobs are non-existent or inadequate to support a family. The big words don't help small towns that can no longer depend upon the numbers of rural people to support existing businesses.

The big words don't say that a farmer who has lost his land will have to look for a job in the city or work as a hired hand for the farmer who bought his land.

It is obvious that the nation as a whole does not understand the farm crisis, nor the ramifications of what farming will be like as larger companies become ever larger and have more and more control over all aspects of farming from seeding to harvesting, from processing to marketing. We can't predict, we can only guess, how consolidations will affect the future availability of food and the prices we will pay for it.

At this time, food is still available. Food is still affordable. The consumer doesn't know or care that the price paid for a single box of cereal is more than the farmer receives for a bushel of grain. The consumer doesn't know that the farmer's costs exceed income and that he is in debt up to his ears and is in danger of losing his land.

What does all of this mean for farmers and small communities caught in the middle of a system not necessarily of their own making? How can they adjust and adapt?

They will have to learn to think outside the box. They will need to explore new approaches to earning a living. Changing a lifestyle is not easy now and it never has been. People are comfortable with the status quo and change can be frightening.

But Dakota people have always been known for their courage, determination, ingenuity, and resourcefulness. It would be my guess that they will rise to meet the challenges ahead, because they know the meaning of those big words.

To order additional copies of
Country-Fied
please complete the following.

$14.95 each *(plus $2.50 shipping & handling)*

Please send me _____ additional books at $ _____ each

Shipping and Handling costs for larger quantites available upon request.

Bill my: ❏ VISA ❏ MasterCard   Expires _____

Card # _____

Signature _____

Daytime Phone Number _____

For credit card orders call 1-888-568-6329

OR SEND THIS ORDER FORM TO:
McCleery & Sons Publishing
PO Box 248
Gwinner, ND 58040-0248

I am enclosing $_____
❏ Check ❏ Money Order

Payable in US funds. No cash accepted.

SHIP TO:

Name_____

Mailing Address _____

City _____

State/Zip _____

Orders by check allow longer delivery time.
Money order and credit card orders will be shipped within 48 hours.
This offer is subject to change without notice.

Other Books Published by
McCleery & Sons Publishing and J&M Companies
visit MCCLEERY & SONS PUBLISHING BOOK STORE at
www.jmcompanies.com

Charlie's Gold and Other Frontier Tales
Kamron's first collection of short stories gives you adventure tales about men and women of the west, made up of cowboys, Indians, and settlers. Written by Kent Kamron. (174 pgs.)
$15.95 each in paper back. (plus $3.50 shipping & handling)

A Time For Justice
This second collection of Kamron's short stories takes off where the first volume left off, satisfying the reader's hunger for more tales of the wide praire.
Written by Kent Kamron. (182 pgs.)
$16.95 each in paper back. (plus $3.50 shipping & handling)

Bonanza Belle
In 1908, Carrie Amundson left her home to become employed on a bonanza farm. One tragedy after the other befell her and altered her life considerably and she found herself back on the farm. Written by Elaine Ulness Swenson. (344 pgs.)
$15.95 each in paper back.
(plus $2.50 ea. shipping & handling)

First The Dream
This story spans ninety years of Anna's life. She finds love, loses it, and finds in once again. A secret that Anna has kept is fully revealed at the end of her life.
Written by Elaine Ulness Swenson. (326 pgs.)
$15.95 each in paper back.
(plus $2.50 ea. shipping & handling)

Pete's New Family
Pete's New Family is a tale for children (ages 4-8) lovingly written to help youngsters understand events of divorce that they are powerless to change. Written by Brenda Jacobson.
$9.95 each in paper back.
(plus $2.50 each shipping & handling)
(price breaks after qty. of 10)

COMING SOON . . .

Honey, I Shrunk the Farm
Dr. Val Farmer's first volume in a three part series on Rural Life is a frank look at the common toils of Farm Economics, Hard Times On The Farm, Coping With Hard Times, Dealing with Debt and Transitions Out of Farming. Written by Val Farmer.

Pay Dirt
Otis Hahn's absorbing story reveals how a man with the courage to follow his dream found both gold and unexpected adventure and adversity in Interior Alaska, while learning that human nature can be the most unpredictable of all. Written by Otis Hahn.